PRIMARY 5 & 6

Tips and Tricks for Creative Writing

Words, Camera, Action!

WS Education

NEW JERSEY • LONDON • SINGAPORE • BEIJING • SHANGHAI • TAIPEI • CHENNAI

Published by

WS Education, an imprint of
World Scientific Publishing Co. Pte. Ltd.
5 Toh Tuck Link, Singapore 596224
USA office: 27 Warren Street, Suite 401-402, Hackensack, NJ 07601
UK office: 57 Shelton Street, Covent Garden, London WC2H 9HE

National Library Board, Singapore Cataloguing in Publication Data
Name(s): Ong, Matthew. | Ooi, Mark, author. | Ong, Jean, author. | Bay, Alan, illustrator.
Title: Words, camera, action! Primary 5 & 6 / by Matthew Ong, Mark Ooi, Jean Ong ;
illustrated by Alan Bay.
Other Title(s): Tips and tricks for creative writing.
Description: Singapore : WS Education, [2025]
Identifier(s): ISBN 978-981-98-1119-9 (paperback)
Subject(s): LCSH: English language--Composition and exercises--Study and teaching (Primary)--
Juvenile literature. | Creative writing (Primary education)--Juvenile literature.
Classification: DDC 372.623--dc23

British Library Cataloguing-in-Publication Data
A catalogue record for this book is available from the British Library.

Printed in Malaysia

Contents

Introduction

Dear Reader,

It's wonderful to see you again! In this book, we will dive deeper into the exciting world of writing and explore new strategies to help you become a more creative and confident writer.

But first, let me introduce you to some very special friends. Don is an aspiring movie director, while Alice is a budding artist. Poppins loves writing poems and spending time outdoors. Like you, they are all keen to learn more about writing and expressing themselves well.

Just the other day, while we were watching Don directing a short film, I overheard Alice asking a truly interesting question:
I use the English language all the time. I read books, watch movies and even dream in English. So why do I find writing compositions so hard?

That question struck me. Why do some students find writing compositions so difficult, even when they read and speak English every day? Well, it turns out that writing well does not just involve knowing and using the language. It's about knowing the right questions to ask, organising your thoughts, expressing your ideas clearly and creating a meaningful story. In fact, many of these thought processes are also relevant to professionals like movie directors and screenwriters!

Sometimes, students get discouraged because they are not able to express themselves or do well in school.

So the first thing that I want to assure you is that you can do it! There is a writer in all of us who is brimming with exciting experiences and interesting ideas. Remember, there is only one you in this whole wide world and that makes your voice very special indeed.

In this book, we will explore some very important ideas for composition writing and reflect on how we can learn to write better. Imagine that you're the director of a blockbuster movie. Before you do anything, you would need to create a great plan of what you want to achieve. This includes asking the right questions and thinking about how the plot, characters, setting, problems and resolutions come together.

Imagine leaving a treasure for others to find in the future: A gem of an idea or a wonderful story you experienced. That's what your writing can be for others – precious treasure hidden within the pages. Believe in your ideas and more importantly, believe in yourself.

Keep dreaming, keep writing!

Yours truly,
Coach

P.S. Oh, I almost forgot! I'm not sure if Spy and his pesky partner Agent Y are still around, but do watch out for them too! They might try to mess things up now and then...

Don

Poppins

Alice

CHAPTER 1

Answering the Right Question

Unless you count the long queues and the waiting!
But isn't that more of an experience, rather than a challenge?
Oh dear... that must be the reason for the question in large bold font then: 'Did you read the topic carefully?'
Don't worry, Don. We all make that mistake from time to time.
Hey, Don, name me a capital.
B!
Huh? I meant a capital city!
B
He gave you a capital all right!
Sure, it is! Look, capital 'B'!
This is an important lesson for us to pay careful attention to the question. This is especially important in your compositions!
I guess I went OOP!
You mean oops?
Nope! O-O-P. Out of point!

Activity 1

Read these two passages and decide which one is relevant to the topic.

Topic: The Day Everything Changed

Passage 1

It was a normal Wednesday morning. Nathan trudged slowly to school with his eyes fixed on the ground. He did not have many friends in school and often felt as though he was invisible. No one seemed to notice him, and he quite liked that feeling at times.

However, everything changed during the school assembly that day. While the entire school was gathered in the hall, the school principal walked solemnly onto the stage and read out the results of the recent Inter-school Writing Competition. After reading out the criteria for the award, he then announced that Nathan from Primary 6.5 had won!

Nathan was stunned as he did not expect an essay he secretly wrote during recess to win such a prestigious award. The school erupted in applause and everyone looked around to see who this 'Nathan' was. That day, when Nathan walked home, he was no longer the invisible boy. Everyone knew who he was, as no one from the school had ever won this award. For the first time, Nathan felt part of the school.

Passage 2

It was a normal Wednesday morning. Nathan trudged slowly to school with his eyes fixed on the ground. He thought about all the different competitions that he had won over the years. He liked that feeling and wondered if he would be able to win yet another award in school that semester.

While the entire school was gathered in the hall, the school principal walked solemnly onto the stage and read out the results of the recent Inter-school Writing Competition. After reading out the criteria for the award, he then announced that Nathan from Primary 6.5 had won!

Nathan was delighted as he had won yet another prestigious award. The school erupted in applause and congratulated Nathan enthusiastically. They were proud to have such a bright student as their schoolmate. That day, when Nathan walked home, he thought about the National Math Olympiad, which was the following week.

Compare and Contrast the Two Passages

	Passage 1	Passage 2
Two similarities in the two passages		
Two differences in the two passages		
Compare how Nathan felt at the start of the passage and at the end		

Which passage do you think is directly relevant to the topic 'The Day Everything Changed'? What makes you say that?

Analysing the Topic

Look at the table below and think about the different topics.

Topic	What it is	What it is not	What objects / pictures come to mind?	What values come to mind?
A challenge	To participate in a **competitive** or **difficult** situation. To threaten someone's position.	An experience that is not difficult or competitive. A casual conversation with someone.	 	Resilience Excellence Determination
A secret	Something that is not known or seen. Something that is not meant to be known or seen by others.	A common fact that everyone is aware of. Something that is easily accessible and obvious to everyone.	 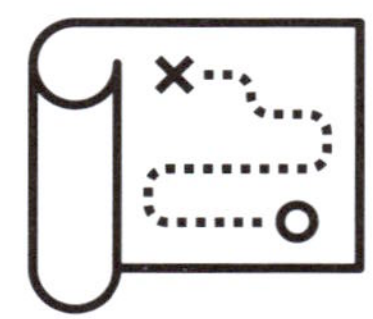	Integrity Unity
Being honest	Being truthful and free of deception. Having integrity and sincerity.	Being kind and giving up a seat on the train. Being courteous and greeting others in the morning.	 	Integrity Truthfulness Righteous

Key Concepts

S.C.O.R.E.

	Key questions	Thoughts	Example for the topic 'Something I Lost'
Study the topic	What is this topic about? What is this topic **not** about?	Read the topic out loud. Think about any prior experiences you might have had.	I lost my phone in a shopping centre. I was with my parents, and they warned me to take care of my belongings because I was rather careless.
Create ideas	What are some synonyms, images, sounds, that come to mind? What is the character transformation like, if any? What are the key themes and values in the story?	List all the ideas that come to mind that are related to the topic. List down all the thoughts and feelings related to the topic.	I regretted not paying attention to my surroundings and heeding my parents' advice. I would learn about the importance of responsibility as some things and memories cannot be replaced. Thoughts and feelings: Scared, worried, angry, upset, anxious...
Organise	What are the main parts of your story?	Draw a mind map with the key story parts (characters, setting, problem and resolution). List the key events in a simple comic strip or a storyboard.	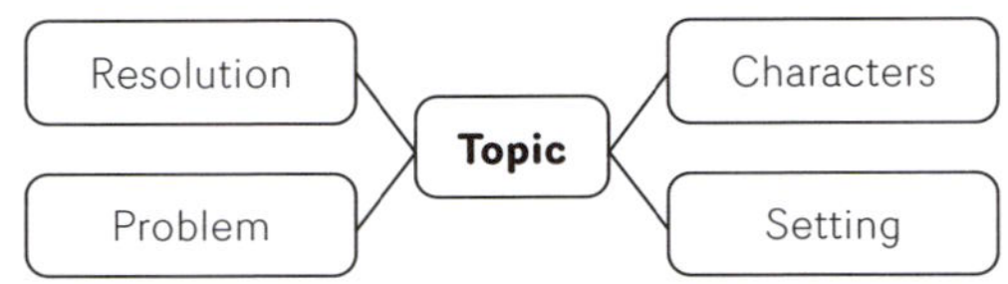 You can use this basic mind map before listing your characters, describing the setting, problem and resolution.
Relevance check	Is my story clearly relevant to the topic?	Read the topic again and study your mind map or plan. Is it directly relevant?	The storyline is directly relevant because I lost my phone.
Evaluate	Are my ideas relevant, interesting and developed enough? How can I improve it further?	Does my story have any unique perspectives? Why is my story worth reading?	Although the storyline is directly relevant, I could explore the deeper meaning behind losing or gaining something too. For example, I lost my phone but learnt about the importance of responsibility.

Practice

Look at the table below and think about the different topics.

Topic	What it is	What it is not	What objects / pictures come to mind?	What values come to mind?
Something precious				
Turning over a new leaf				
Someone special				

Puzzle Time 1

Across	Clue
2	Miserable
3	Opposite of shout
6	Believing
7	Consume
9	Sprint

Down	Clue
1	Opposite of Satisfied
4	Continue
5	Chief
8	Opposite of Nomad
10	Opposite of Capture

Answers: Puzzle Time 1

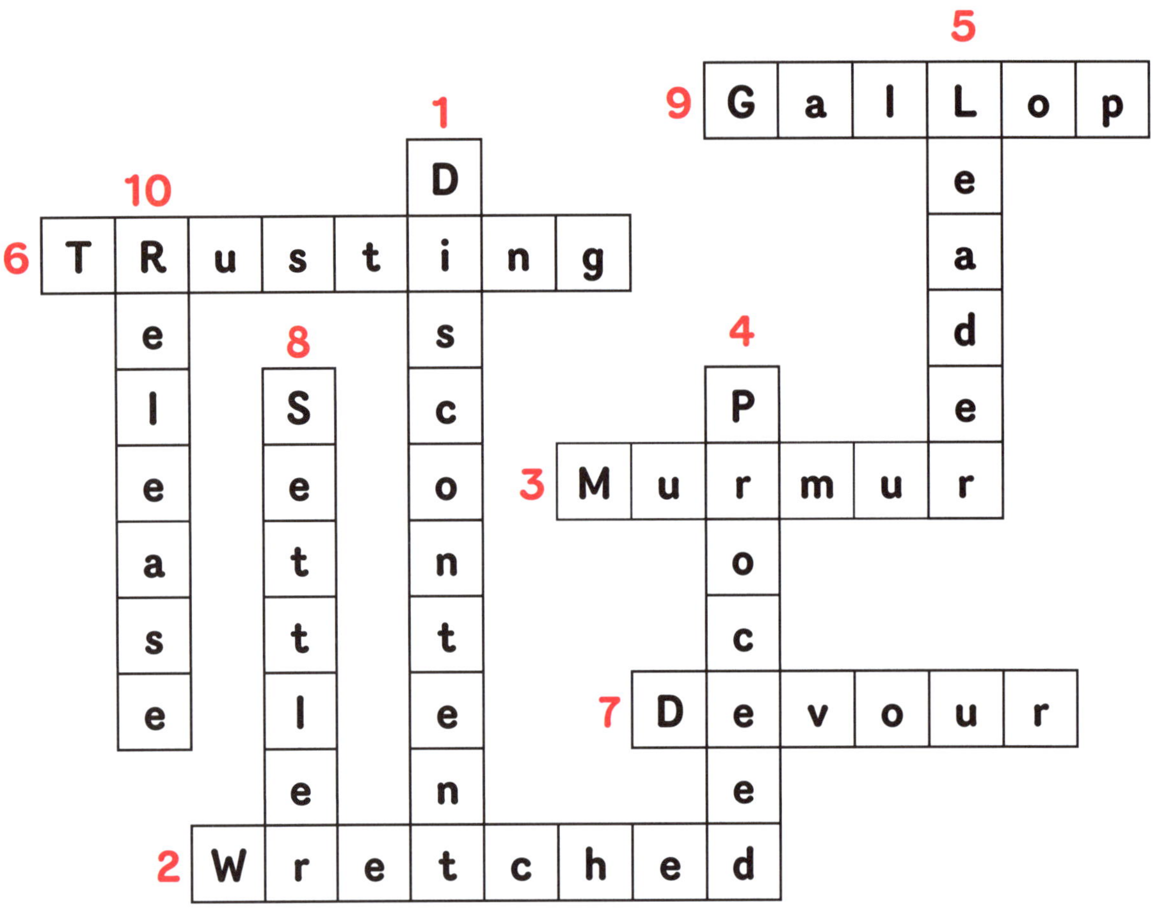

A Poem for You

Coco studied all night and felt quite bright.
She had prepared for the quiz and felt alright.
The question was about the inventor of the lightbulb,
but she talked about the importance of lightbulbs.

The judge blinked and his confusion grew,
"That's not the question, though what you've said is true."
Coco raised her hands and gave a whoop,
but the judge pressed the buzzer to signal a bloop.

Coco learnt an important lesson that day.
Although she had interesting answers to say,
she had to listen to the question at hand,
or wind up with a big egg on hand.

CHAPTER 2

Fail to Plan, Plan to Fail

Wow, could you both share a little more?
Well, I like writing poems and that's a lot shorter than a full essay or novel. I use sticky notes to write down my most important ideas.
I find it helpful to write down the themes on red sticky notes, followed by the feelings or mood on blue sticky notes and then the settings on green ones. I like writing down great phrases and words for the rich descriptions too.
Wow, your plans sound great! Unfortunately, I don't really have a fixed way to plan my artwork. I simply make sure that my worktable is clean the night before and all my materials are laid out on the table.
Wow, why do you do that the night before?
Well, once I start, I can get going very quickly. I set quite a strict routine for myself during the weekends when I'm painting too. I'll spend about an hour sketching my artwork first. This is in pencil, so I can erase it if it isn't nice. After that, I can start painting the outlines for the next hour or so. I usually set a fixed time to start and stop my work.
So, you're planning the drawing process and the time that you will put in. That's fantastic because people often neglect this part of planning.
You mean like the time and routines?
Exactly. We can't draw mind maps or outline storyboards if we don't have the time and materials, right?
Hmmm... maybe that's why I take such a long time to produce my work. I must plan my time better!
So, you have all outlined some very nice ideas that we can use for our planning today! You can use mind maps, storyboards and sticky notes to plan what you want to write in your compositions. You could write down the overall story parts like characters, setting, problem and resolutions before outlining the whole plot in the storyboard.
You know, one of my friends, Bernard, is a musician. He often records his musical pieces to listen to how they sound like. Perhaps we could audio record our stories on a device, before writing them out.
That's a great idea! Often, when I read out my essay or talk about my plan, I find new ways of improving it.
Wonderful! Sounds like we have a plan for moving ahead with our essay topic for today!
Let's get down to it!

Key Concepts

Planning is crucial because it allows us to have greater clarity and focus on our writing. It also enables us to think carefully about the topic and the task that we need to complete.

Planning does not only involve thinking about the task and the topic. It can also help us to set clear goals and objectives for the task. For example, we may wish to learn a particular strategy for writing and apply it in our work. This may also help us to identify the challenges involved and ways to overcome them.

Planning also helps us to monitor our progress and analyse the way that we approach the task. In this way, if we do not succeed, we can return to the plan and adjust certain aspects to improve. If we manage to complete the task, we can still analyse the plan to see how to improve on the performance even more.

There are several ways that we can plan an essay.

Methods	Short description of using this method
Mind maps	Mind maps can help us to present our ideas and structure them in a clear diagram. We can link related ideas and expand on them easily. Mind maps are especially useful for identifying a key theme and then building on the different parts to form a comprehensive story.
Storyboards	Storyboards are useful methods to plan the flow and sequence of the story. By using different frames for each key scene, we can see how the events develop and how they fit together logically. Just think about your plan in the form of a comic strip!

Sketches and visual notes	Sketches and visual notes can be useful ways to stimulate more creativity and help you see how the ideas may be connected too. You may draw images or write text on these notes to analyse the topic and form connections between ideas. This may also be converted into a mind map later if you have enough details and connections between the points.
Audio notes	We can make audio notes by reading out a key scene and then recording it. When we read it out, we are also listening to what the story sounds like and whether it flows. It forces us to analyse the story and think about whether it works. Audio notes can be useful to capture thoughts quickly.
Digital tools	There are numerous digital tools that will allow you to do many of the methods above online. By completing your mind maps, storyboards, sketches and audio notes online, it can help you to capture your thoughts and ideas easily for reference in the future.

MIND MAP

Key terms	Short description	Example below
Main idea	This refers to the main theme in the story	Being truthful
Story parts	This refers to the character, setting and events	Characters, setting, problem and resolution
Story details	This refers to the specific details about the story parts	Details for characters: Adam and Bruce
Connections	Story links and how they form the bigger picture	The lines, which are like branches
Story map	The overall picture with the story parts, details and connections	The whole map below

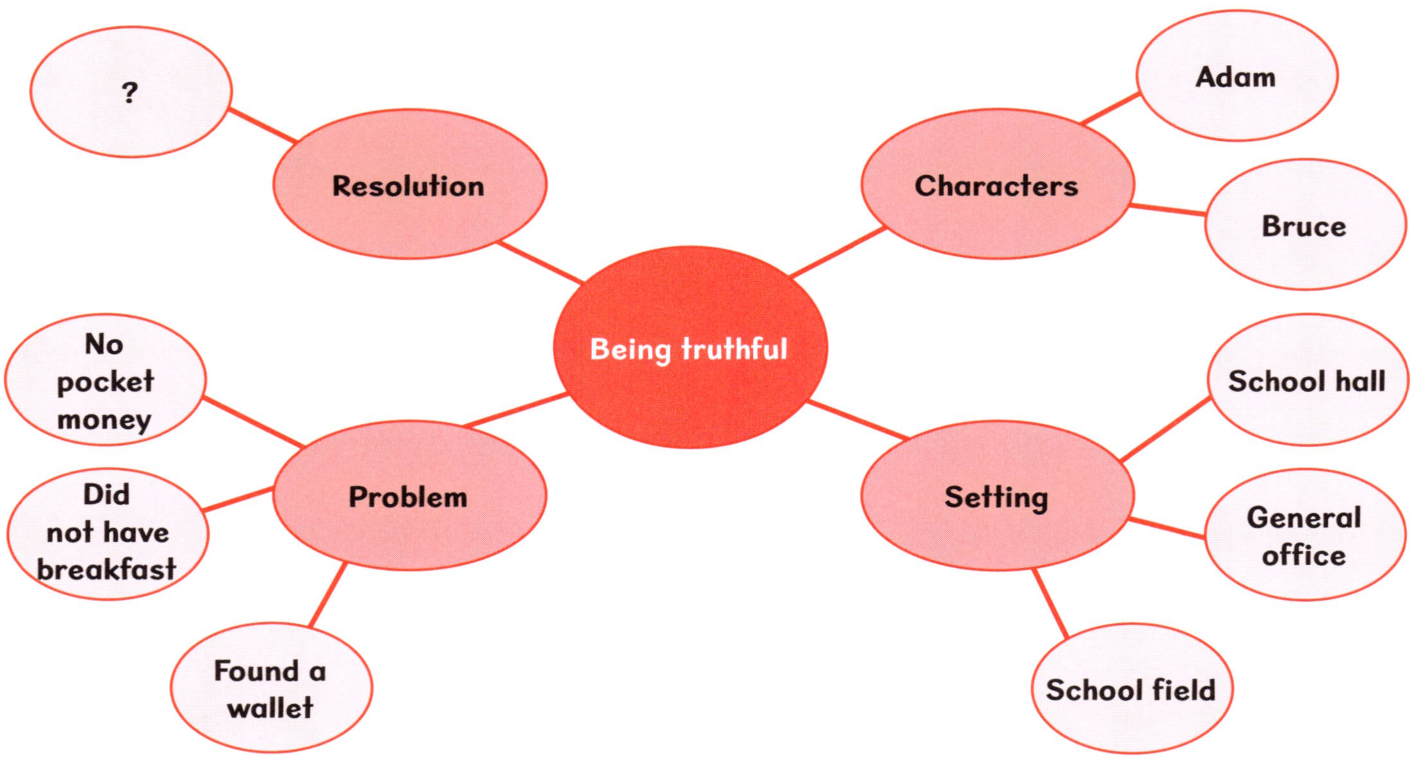

STORY-LOGICAL TIMELINE

Think about what will happen in your story. In the space below, draw a timeline and add details showing the events that occur in your story in chronological sequence. An example has been done for you below.

STORY-LOGICAL TIMELINE

Your turn!

Think about what will happen in your story. In the timeline below, draw lines and add details showing the events that occur in your story in chronological sequence. Share it with your friends!

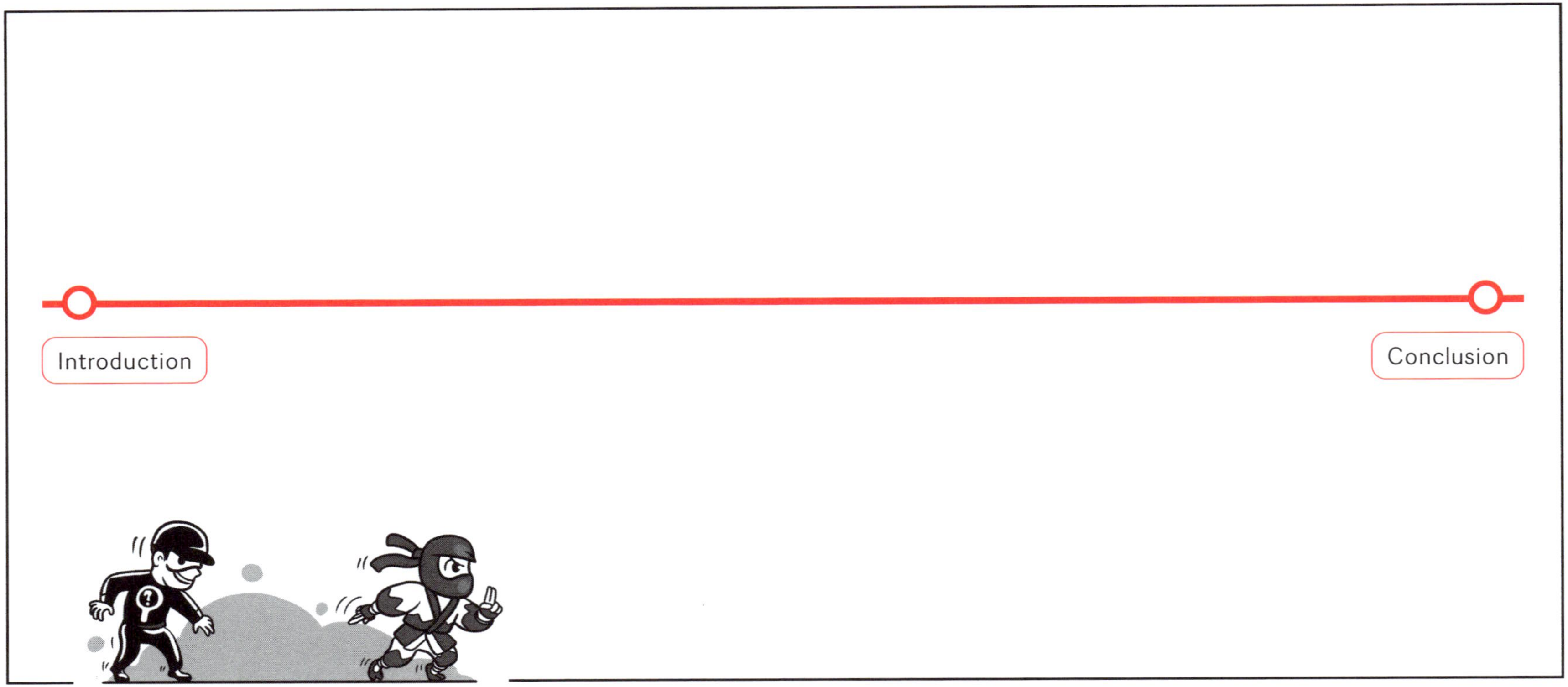

Puzzle Time 2

Across	Clue
1	Opposite of assemble
4	Stronghold
6	Astonish
7	Rent
8	Opposite of release
9	Talk

Down	Clue
2	Content
3	Yell
5	Distrustful
10	Follower

Answers: Puzzle Time 2

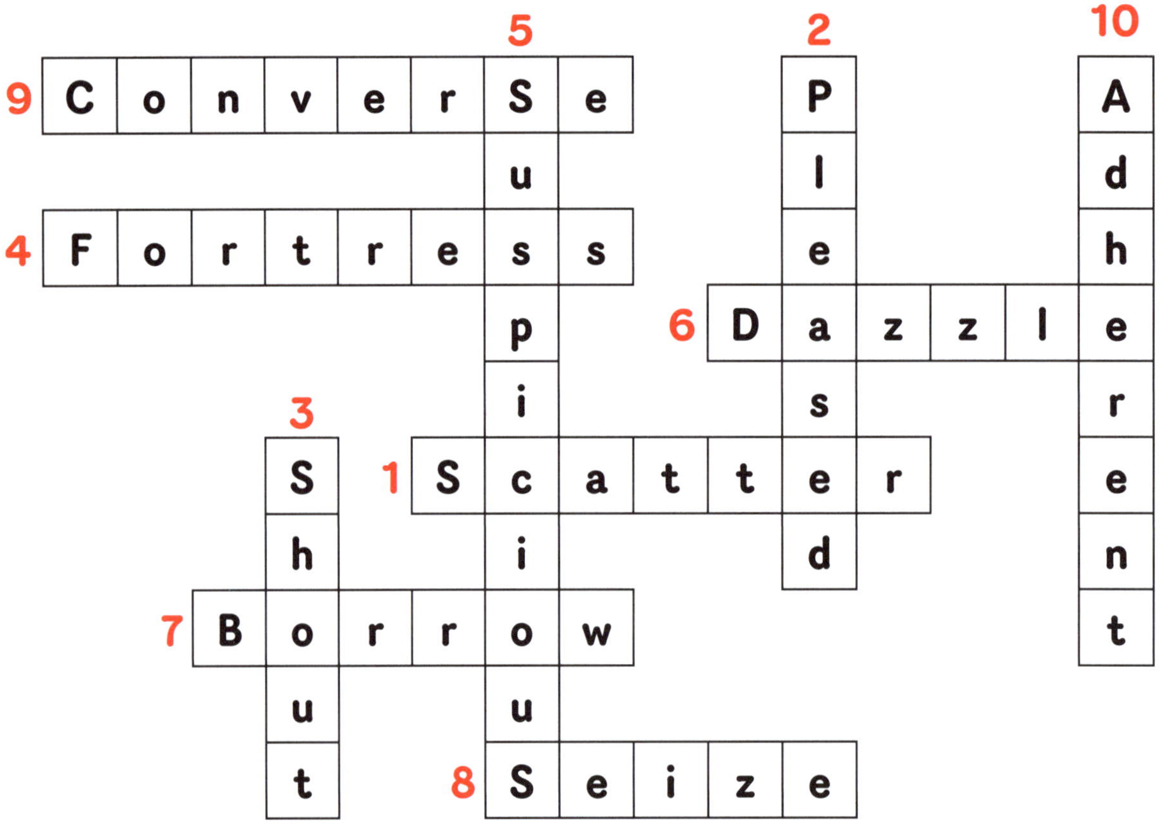

A Song About Planning

Went to bed last night thinking I was the boss.
But I got up this morning feeling a little lost.
I didn't have a plan and couldn't find my phone.
I kept running around in circles and really should have known.

I've got to write this essay, but I'm stuck.
My mind's gone blank, and my ideas are lame ducks.

But wait, wait, wait. No need for such dismay.
I've got just the thing to save the day!

Grab those markers and let's write down a plan.
Don't you panic, I'm the one with the plan.

Mind maps, storyboards, sticky little notes.
I've got them all and will stay afloat.

I'm going to plan it out and not be lazy.
When all is set, my writing won't be hazy.
I'll get this done before I go crazy!

CHAPTER 3

Lights, Camera, Action!

How's this for 'A Secret'?
How my heart frets when I learn new secrets. Some things are better not known, especially if they make you groan!
These are great ideas! But what about 'A Difficult Task'?
I'd have an actress playing a gymnast and falling repeatedly while she's trying to complete a routine. She's a national athlete and is determined to perfect a very difficult routine.
I remember my Primary 5 camp! That was the hardest challenge for me... I was so scared!
I don't know, folks. Writing is a difficult enough task for me!
Everything is hard when you slack and laze around! Come on, Agent Y, let's get cracking!

MIND MAP

Mind maps are a wonderful way to visualise your story in a picture. In the mind map below, write down the different ideas you might have about the topic on 'Learning Something New'. You can add new bubbles and connection lines.

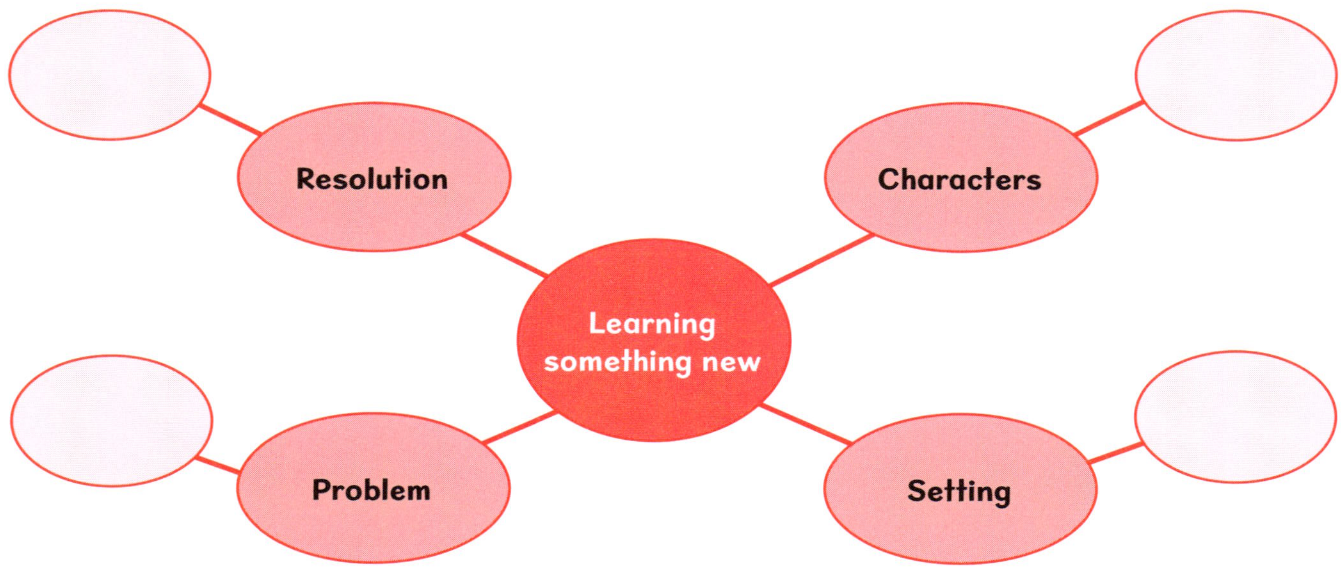

STORYBOARDING WITH DON

Alright everyone, you'll now have a chance to draw and sequence your story using the eight frames below. Every good movie that you have watched would have been planned out carefully. Each of these movies usually have a storyboard. Some of them can involve hundreds and thousands of frames! Using the mind map as your overall plan, draw your story in the frames below.

Frame 1

Frame 2

Frame 3

Frame 4

Frame 5

Frame 6

Frame 7

Frame 8

A Word is Worth a Thousand Pictures with Alice

When you think about the following topics, what pictures come to mind? Alice has shared some of her favourite pictures. You can share yours too!

Topic	Sample picture	Draw your picture here
An act of courage	 A fireman who is courageous when he saves others in a fire.	
A challenge	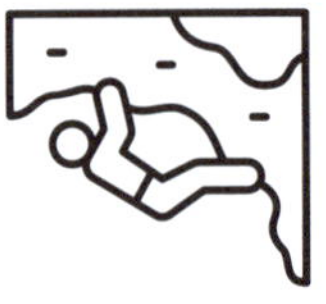 Rock climbing during an outdoor camp for the first time.	
A painful lesson	 Fracturing my leg after cycling down a slope.	
A best friend	 Writing to my best friend who is overseas.	
A secret	 A secret room which has not been opened in years. You found the key. Should you open the room?	

Key Concepts

You can think about the topic and pictures using these five modes. Please note that not all the modes may be useful for every composition activity, and some may be used more easily than others. The table below shows how you might be able to think about these modes and use them for your creative expression!

Mode	Key ideas	Question to think about as you read the composition topic	Possible examples/activities for a topic on 'A challenge'
Visual	This refers to the images and colour.	What images come to mind? How can these images be used in your writing?	First, draw or search for an image that truly captures the topic on 'A Challenge'. Describe the image in as much detail as you can. 'Jim's perspiration dripped down his forehead. His eyes stared narrowly at the finish line. Crouching down at the starting block, he looked like a loaded spring ready to burst ahead.'
Linguistic	This refers to the words and language used. It can refer to both the written and spoken words.	What words come to mind? What synonyms and metaphors can you use to describe the setting?	Resilience, excellence, failure, courage A hurdle could mean two things. It could be an object you must jump over or a metaphor for something you have to overcome.
Gestures	This refers to the body language and facial expression.	How would your character's body language reflect their emotions? What could your character's facial expression show that their words cannot?	Watch a short clip of your favourite cartoon or movie but turn down the volume. Study their body language and how they walk or behave. Can you describe this scene in detail in your story? 'Jim grimaced in pain as he stumbled over the final hurdle. Clenching his teeth and squinting his eyes, he continued to stare at the finishing line. His coach smiled as he could tell from Jim's expression that he was not going to give up.'

Mode	Key ideas	Question to think about as you read the composition topic	Possible examples/activities for a topic on 'A challenge'
Touch 	This refers to the sense of touch and physical contact.	Is there an object that might capture the meaning of the topic? How would that object feel like?	Think about the most important objects in a particular scene of your composition. How would it feel to touch these objects and what would they feel like? 'Jim ran his fingers over the cool and smooth silver trophy. He studied its grooves and smiled at the small carvings on the wooden base which now bore his name.'
Hearing 	This refers to the sound, music and silence.	If your story had a soundtrack, what would it be? What would be some of the key sounds in the key scenes in your story?	Think about the sounds in your story and how they would affect the setting and characters. How would you describe them? 'The crowd erupted with a deafening roar that thundered across the stadium. The spectators cheered loudly and whistled in admiration for the athlete who fell and yet managed to complete the race. They pounded their feet in awe and started chanting his name.'

Puzzle Time 3

Across	Clue
3	Spectator
4	Opposite of dull
7	Bitter
8	Opposite of observer
9	Unhappy
10	Overjoyed

Down	Clue
1	Despondent
2	Lure
5	Create
6	Opposite of confident

Answers: Puzzle Time 3

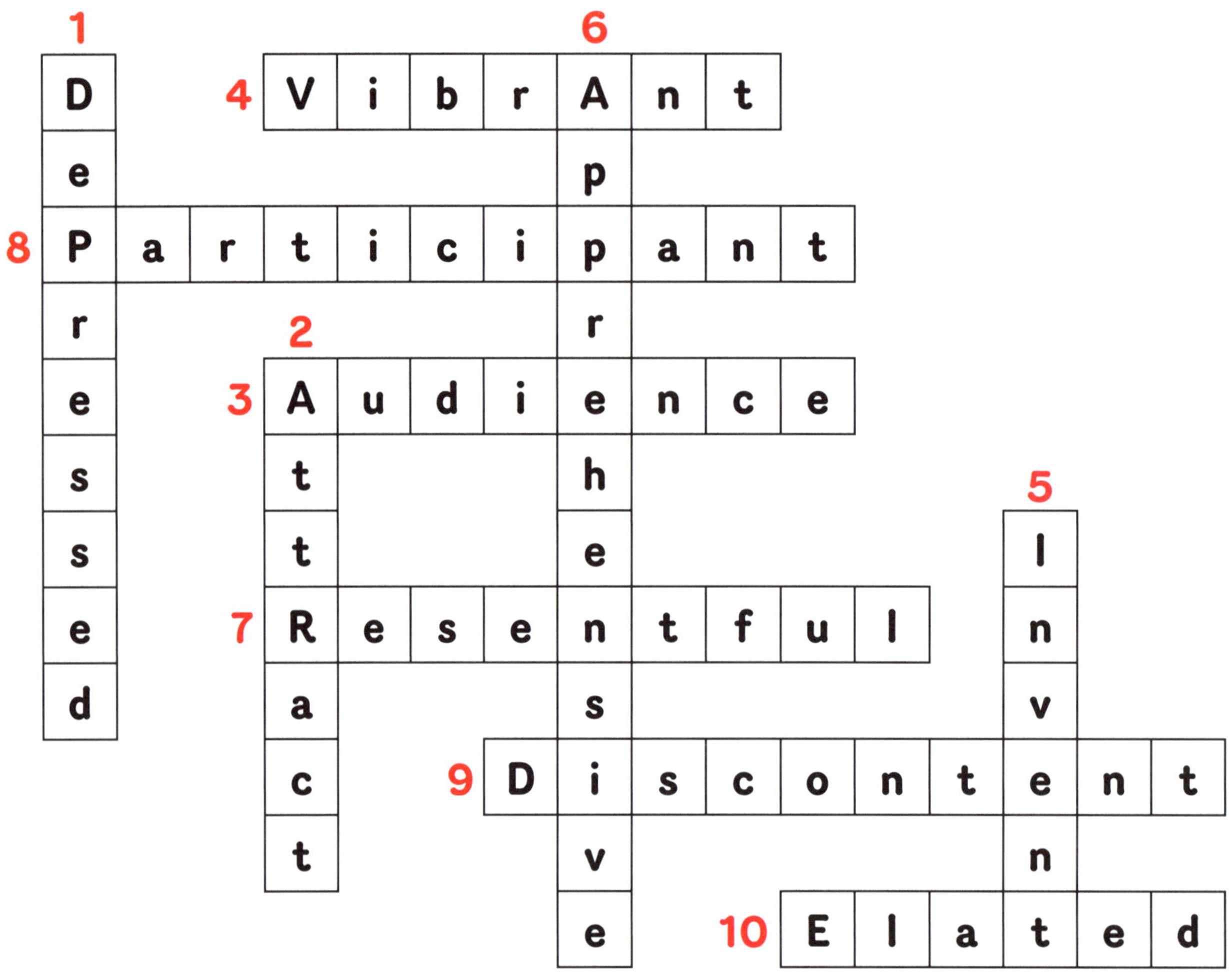

Poem About the Senses

To the tune of
"Twinkle, Twinkle Little Star"

Watch the waves as they unfold.

Listen to the children laugh.

Taste the salt in a sea breeze.

Feel the sand under your feet.

Smell the smoky barbeque.

How I love my holidays!

- Coach

CHAPTER 4

Thinking About Thinking

There are three ways that we can help ourselves to become better writers.
You're not going to say write, write and write some more, are you?
The practice is certainly important but no, Don. It's about leading and helping ourselves. What do you think would be important ways that we can help ourselves to improve?
I think that setting goals would be very important!
Strategies! I often try out different strategies for my poems and see if they work. If they do, I keep using them. If they don't, and people don't respond to my poems, I stop using them.
I usually use different formats like text, visual and auditory modes to test out the ideas for my movies. However, the key is to test it out and get feedback from others in the team too.
Wonderful! You've mentioned some great ideas and pointed out that it's very important to try it out to get feedback from others. This process of constantly improving based on the feedback is what makes these reflection skills so powerful.
What about preparing the table the night before? My mother always tells me to keep my table and painting area clean.
My table is always messy!
That's why you take so long to get started!
Well, I'll have to improve on that!
One of the most important things that I often do is to read my poems out loud after I'm done. It helps me to listen to how it sounds like. I then ask myself how I might react if I was listening to the poem.
Reading your work out loud is certainly a very powerful way to check and improve your writing! Alright everyone, let's use some of these worksheets to guide our own reflection processes!
Let's go!

I would like to plan and set clear goals for my writing. There are so many things to think about though. Where should we start?
We should start small. I think we should set goals that are meaningful and achievable for ourselves. It could be something as simple as ensuring that the composition is highly related to the task. It could also be using a new strategy that you will learn from one of the later chapters.
What about other things, like organising our writing and time management?
It can get quite overwhelming when you think of all the things you need to plan. Here are some of the things to think about.
Plans that are related to the task:
1. Mind maps to brainstorm for ideas.
2. Storyboards to arrange the flow of the ideas.
3. Checklists to ensure that your essay is related to the task.
Plans that are related to the environment:
1. Checklists to think about how your writing environment is suitable for you.
Plans that are related to monitoring your performance:
1. A progress monitoring chart or checklist.
2. You could also have rewards to inspire you to achieve your goals!
Wow, this sounds like a plan!
There are so many ways to sabotage their work here, Agent Y.
Oh yes, we can mess up their plans, their checklists or even their monitoring charts!
If they don't plan or think about their own work, there's no chance they will write well.
Finally... something that we can succeed in messing up!
Let's start our own plan now!

Figuring Out My Current Writing Style and Methods

Questions	Your responses	Your reflections on your own responses. What will you continue doing and what will you seek to improve?
Do you set any goals before writing your essay? Why?		
Do you spend time planning? Describe how you plan.		
Do you think about your writing space and how it might affect your writing?		
How do you reflect on each essay and think about the areas to improve?		

Ways I Can Help Myself Become a Better Writer: Setting Goals

Think about a writing activity. What are some of the key goals that you would like to set for yourself? Why?

My writing activity *What is your writing activity?*	My goal *What do you want to achieve?*	My reason *Why do you want to achieve this?*	My reflections *What are your reflections after you have done the work?*
Don's example: *Planning for an engaging introduction.*	*To be able to write an introduction using the flashback technique with a meaningful object as the trigger for the memory.*	*Objects can be powerful triggers for memories.*	*I was able to use an object to trigger a character's memory. It was relevant to the task and meaningful.* *I could have done better to describe the object though.*

Ways I Can Help Myself Become a Better Writer: Organising My Writing

Think about a writing activity. How can you create ideas and organise them in your writing? Why?

My writing activity ***What is your writing activity?***	**My goal** ***What do you want to achieve?***	**My reason** ***Why do you want to achieve this?***	**My reflections** ***What are your reflections after you have done the work?***
Alice's example: *Brainstorming for ideas for my essay and organising them.*	*To be able to use a mind map to generate ideas (character, setting, problem and resolution) and organise my ideas.*	*Mind maps help me to visualise my ideas and see how they are connected to one another.*	*I was able to describe the main story parts such as the character, setting, problem and resolution. However, I realised that the problem was not meaningful enough.*

Ways I Can Help Myself Become a Better Writer: Designing My Writing Space

Think about where you are writing. How will you ensure that it is suitable for writing?

My writing activity *What is your writing activity?*	My goal *What do you want to achieve?*	My reason *Why do you want to achieve this?*	My reflections *What are your reflections after you have done the work?*
Poppins' example: *Prepare my writing table and ensure that it's organised.*	*I want to create a suitable writing space where I can concentrate on my writing.*	*I write best when it is not too noisy and there is sufficient space around me. When it's noisy and the table is messy, I can't concentrate.*	*I was able to organise my table well and prepare all my stationery before writing.*

Self-monitoring Checklist: Task (Example)

Task	Put a check or cross here	Provide details and reflections here. What made you put a check or cross?	Feedback from my peer or teacher	Reflections after receiving the feedback.
My essay was relevant to the task.	✓	I spent time thinking about the topic (a challenge) in the task and ensured that my essay was directly relevant to it. I wrote about something challenging that my protagonist struggled to overcome. In the end, he succeeded.	My teacher highlighted that my essay was relevant to the task so that is good.	I will continue to spend time analysing the topic for a few minutes before planning and then writing.
I was able to check my work thoroughly.	✗	I was able to skim through my essay at the end. However, I was anxious to finish, so I did not check it carefully enough.	My peers shared that there were many grammar and spelling errors.	I will try to set aside more time to check my work after writing. I will read out my essay to check for these common errors.
I was able to use a particular writing strategy in my essay.	✓	I wanted to use a slow-motion technique in my essay .	My teacher shared that this paragraph was very descriptive.	I will continue to use this technique whenever I want to provide a rich description and slow down time for the reader.

Self-monitoring Checklist: Task

Task	Put a check or cross here	Provide details and reflections here. What made you put a check or cross?	Feedback from my peer or teacher	Reflections after receiving the feedback.
My essay was relevant to the task.				
I was able to check my work thoroughly.				
I was able to use a particular writing strategy in my essay.				

Progress monitoring for my writing

Title of composition	Target score	Actual score	Reflections after receiving the feedback.
Don's example: *An Unforgettable Day*	*28*	*26*	*I made quite a few grammar and spelling mistakes that I could have easily avoided. I will need to read my essay carefully at the end to check my work.*

List of Useful Words and Ideas for Thinking About Your Own Thinking

Key terms	Simple description
Self-awareness	To be able to recognise and be aware of your own thinking. *For example: I am aware that I was able to think about the topic carefully and plan my essay.*
Reflections	To think about your own thinking. *For example: I was thinking about how I planned my essay using the mind map. The characters were well designed, but the setting lacked details.*
Self-monitoring	To be able to keep track of your own performance. *For example: I noticed that my language score has not improved over the past few essays. My content score has been going up slowly though.* *OR* *I was able to use different techniques during the planning stage. I was able to use a new technique for every essay.*

Self-questioning	To ask probing questions on why and how you wrote your essay. *For example: Why did I use this particular object for this task? How was it relevant to the topic?*
Thinking strategies	This refers to the different ways we use to think and solve a problem. *For example: I was able to use a mind map to outline the key parts of my essay. I thought of many ideas and put them into my mind map.*
Evaluate	This refers to assessing or thinking about how well you did something. *For example: I was able to use the 'flashback' technique well because the introduction was engaging and my friends wanted to know what happened next.*
Adjust and adapt	This refers to changing your plan based on your thinking or evaluation to improve your performance. *For example: I was not able to complete my essay within the given time frame. I will need to adjust the time I spend on planning and use more time to write my essay.*

Spy and Agent Y's Plan to Sabotage Your Writing

1. Distract you and make sure you do not read the task carefully.

2. If you have read the task, distract you so that you don't think about it deeply. Fool you into thinking that you have answered the question when all you have done is mention the topic.

3. Stop you from planning. This will make your writing disorganised.

4. If you have planned your essay, keep it simplistic and prevent you from writing down too many details. Fool you into thinking that you have a plan or useful mind map when all you have are meaningless words in some bubbles with lines.

5. Keep you inattentive while you are writing. Distract you and make you lose focus.

6. Prevent you from completing your work on time. Tempt you with different things. Make you lose track of time and procrastinate.

7. Make you think that you are smart so that you don't check your work. Fool you into thinking that the essay is completed and that there is no need for checklists or checking your work.

8. Prevent you from tracking your progress. Keep you clueless about how to improve.

9. Stop you from sharing your work with others. Sometimes your peers can give you good feedback.

10. Remind you about how painful writing is and how much effort it takes. Don't let you read the beautiful poems and stories in the world. Keep you in the dark!

___'s 10 Rules for Writing Great Essays

Rule 1: ______________________________

Rule 2: ______________________________

Rule 3: ______________________________

Rule 4: ______________________________

Rule 5: ______________________________

Rule 6: ______________________________

Rule 7: ______________________________

Rule 8: ______________________________

Rule 9: ______________________________

Rule 10: ______________________________

My greatest story is yet to be told!

Puzzle Time 4

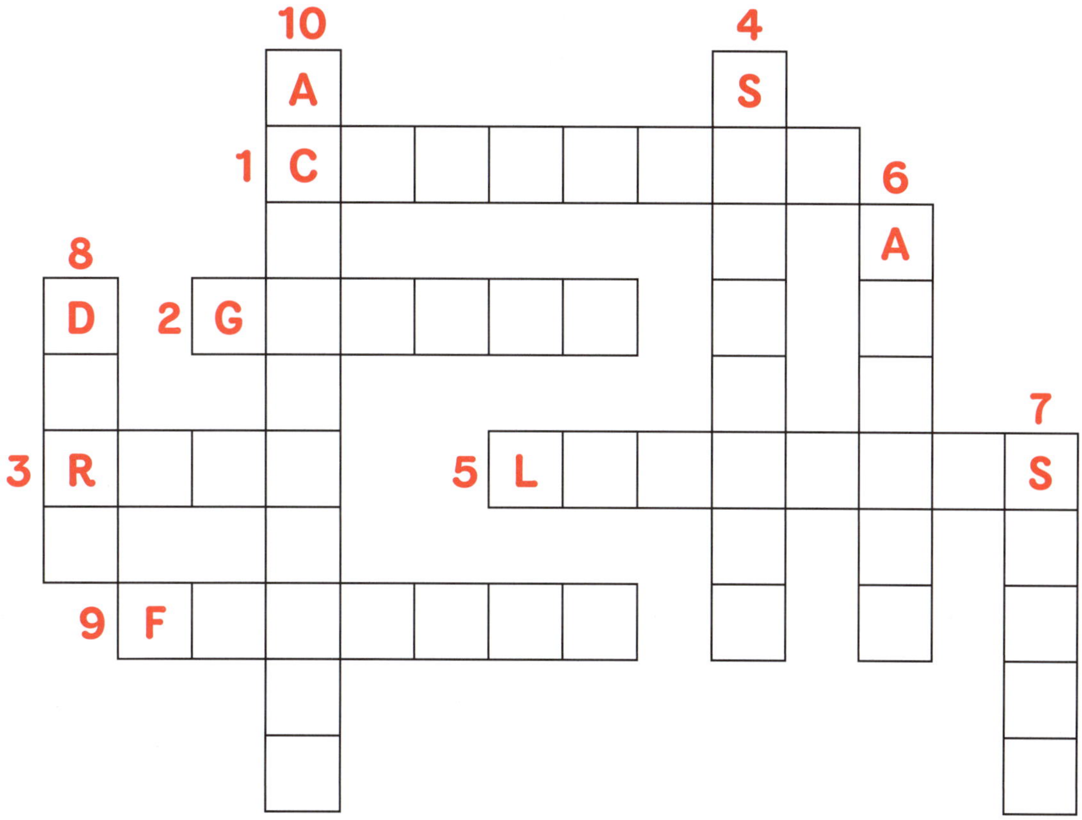

Across	Clue
1	Opposite of courageous
2	Soft
3	Opposite of polite
5	Bright
9	Opposite of brave

Down	Clue
4	Slow
6	Opposite of repel
7	Quick
8	Dim
10	Opposite of decelerate

Answers: Puzzle Time 4

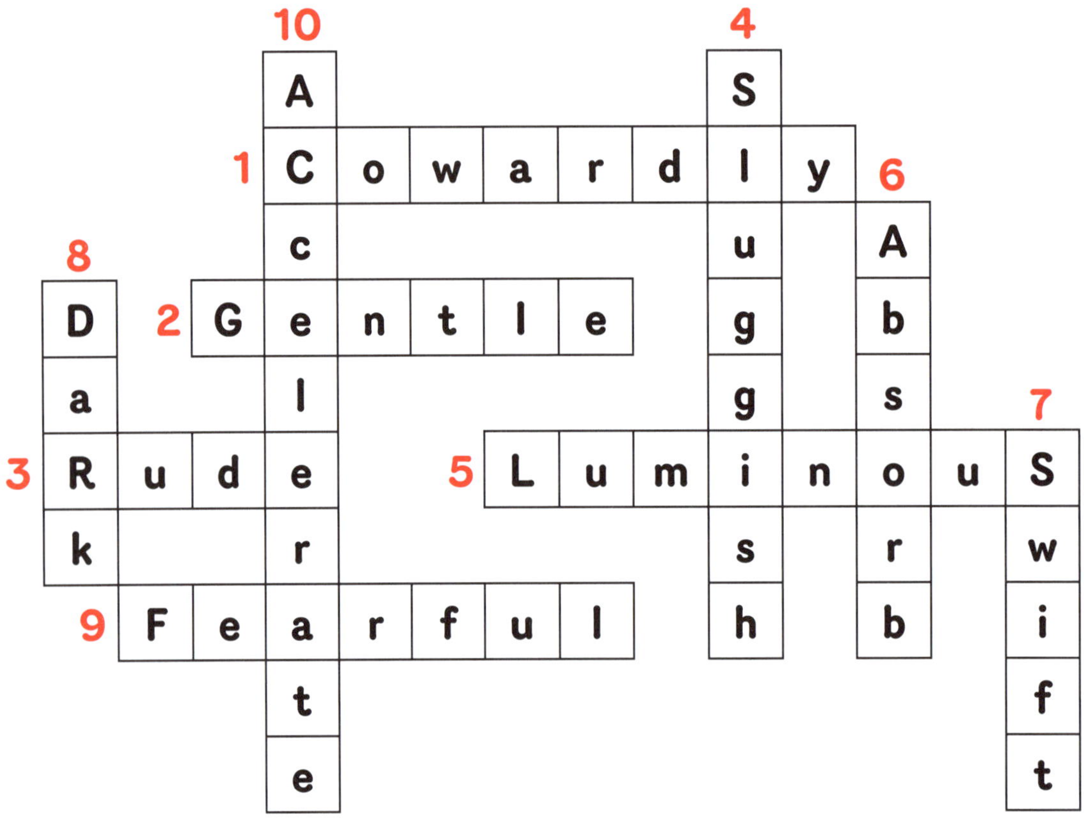

CHAPTER 5

How to Write C.R.I.S.P. Stories Like in the Movies

There's more than meets the eye.
A problem twists, it turns, it questions why.
The deeper roots are where it lies,
and only there the true path flies.
Well put, Poppins. The best stories have layers of problems. Sometimes they start with something obvious. Then, as the plot unfolds, new challenges emerge. Those are the moments where the story deepens, and the audience leans in.
And, the more complicated the problem, the more satisfying the solution. In *Lord of the Rings*, the problem isn't just to 'destroy the ring.' Along the way, Frodo and Sam face betrayal, exhaustion and the growing temptation of the ring's power. Destroying the ring is only meaningful because the journey became so complex.
Right! But how do we do this in our writing?
Think about how the problem evolves. Do your characters face new obstacles as they try to solve the initial issue? Do the stakes get higher? These layers are what make a story so intriguing.
My screenwriters often share that when the solution is too easy, it's not fun to watch or read. It can become boring when the reader can predict exactly what will happen in a story.
The characters should struggle. It is the heart of the story. Think about *Indiana Jones*. The problem is finding the lost artifact, but each step reveals new dangers — traps, enemies, even being betrayed by 'friends'! The development of the problem keeps the excitement going.
It's like solving a puzzle. The more pieces you fit together, the more you realise how complicated the problem was all along.
Exactly! In every story, the problem should grow and shift. This will draw your reader in to want to find out more about the characters and how they overcome the problem!

I get it! When characters face problems that keep changing, it forces them to come up with creative solutions. That's where the fun comes in.
That's true for all forms of art. A great painting, like a great story, reveals new challenges as you work on it, and every stroke is part of solving that problem.
The problem bends, it splits, it breaks. But every shift a new path makes. The solution's found not at the start, but through each challenge, step and heart.
Well said, Poppins! When you're writing, think about how you can make your problems multi-layered. It has to be just right though. Too easy and it's solved too quickly. Too hard and it's never solved — or time runs out!
Yes! The solution is satisfying because of the journey the character went on to overcome the problem.
And a good story, like a good poem, thrives on the problems it faces. The twists and turns lead to the most meaningful endings.
Exactly! So, let's take what we've learned and start thinking about our own stories. What are the problems your characters face? How do those problems grow, and how do they change the story and/or the characters?
What problem shall we create for them, Agent Y?
A problem without a solution!
That sounds awful — for them!
Perfect. Let's steal their solution section then!

Key Concepts

In every captivating story, the problem helps to drive the plot forward. Whether the story is in the form of a movie, a book or a play, the central conflict challenges the characters, pushing them to make decisions, overcome obstacles and ultimately grow.

A well-designed and interesting problem does not just share or state the external events that happen to the characters. For example, needing to find something that was lost, or needing to defeat a formidable enemy.

What makes a problem thoughtfully crafted and intriguing is what happens while the characters try to overcome the problem. It is about the internal struggles they face. As characters grapple with difficult choices, they reveal their fears, desires and strengths. For example, on the way to finding what was lost, how do the characters deal with the fear of failing, the sadness of losing it in the first place or the unforeseen obstacles that pop up along the way? Similarly, in defeating a formidable enemy, how do the characters deal with the fear they might face, their weaknesses or their differences of opinion regarding the battle plan? It is the journey towards solving the problem that makes it an interesting problem.

Similarly, the solution to the problem is not simply a resolution of events. It is a moment of transformation, where the characters have learned something important about themselves, each other or the world. The journey from problem to solution shows how they evolve! This keeps the audience invested in the story.

Remember and apply C.R.I.S.P. to help you craft an interesting problem and solution in your story:

Challenge	The problem should challenge your characters in ways that force them to make tough decisions, which forces them to change or grow. 	**Spy's key questions** How will this problem push the characters out of their comfort zone?
Reactions	Instead of jumping into how the characters go about solving the problem immediately, it is important to show their emotional and mental reactions to the problem. 	**Spy's key questions** How do they feel when faced with this challenge? Show how their internal strengths, weaknesses, and struggles affect them as they face the problem.
Impact	Ma_e the problem matter. An interesting problem __oes not affect only the main character but __lso their relationships, world or future. 	**Spy's key questions** How does solving (or failing to solve) the problem change things? How do the stakes involved force the characters to act?
Solution-finding	Sh__w with vibrant descript__ions how the ch__r__ct__rs d__vise a plan to t__ckle the pr__bl__m. Th__nk about h__w they mi__ht fail, and h__w th__y t__y a__ain. A g__od so__uti__n d__esn't c__me e__sy. 	**Spy's key questions** How does the character's approach to solving the problem change as they fail and try again?
Plan	P__t yo__r id__as alt__geter in a m__nd m__p or a pl__n so that you c__n see h__w the pr__bl__m and s__luti__n f__ts t__get__er.	**Spy's key questions** How does the problem and solution all fit together in the story?

Oh dear! What happened to the solution section?
It appears to have vanished right into the pages!
I suspect someone's playing a prank on us... What shall we do, Coach?
It's alright, everyone. We'll practice by focussing on the challenge first. I'm sure the solution will pop up later on. Let's work on the C.R.I. now.
Let's get down to it!

C.R.I. in Action!

Example:
Captain Galactico is trying to overcome a huge challenge. An alien scientist has unleashed a crazy machine powered by a shooting star. The machines have captured half of all human beings on Earth and sent them to another galaxy. Galactico has to go back in time, hide the fallen shooting star and save everyone. Galactico is afraid of taking risks and worries about making a mistake that could change time forever.

See the table below as an example of how you can apply C.R.I. to create an interesting problem in a story.

Challenge	**Key question:** What challenge does Galactico face? **Possible answer:** Galactico will need to figure out how to time travel, find a way to hide a fallen shooting star and stop the scientist from using his machine. **Key question:** How does the problem force Galactico out of his comfort zone to take action? **Possible answer:** The problem challenges Galactico by forcing him to go out of his comfort zone by taking risks.
Reactions	**Key question:** How does Galactico react emotionally and mentally when faced with this challenge? **Possible answer:** Galactico is afraid of making a mistake, thus he procrastinates and does not dare to try travelling back in time. **Key question:** How does his reaction change as the story goes on? **Possible answer:** Galactico manages to snap himself out of his fearful state. He finds a book given to him by his parents and is reminded about how they were always there for him. The book ended with the words 'You are never alone'.
Impact	**Key question:** How does this problem affect the larger world? What are the stakes of solving this problem? **Answer:** It affects the entire world because half of all human beings will be gone if Galactico fails to stop the alien scientist. Everyone on Earth will be stuck with the grief of their loved ones disappearing forever.

Scenario:

A pair of unlikely heroes, who call themselves the Dream Team, must save a faraway planet from a dangerous villain who plans to steal a powerful artifact. Captain Galactico and Uncle Rajoo must put aside their differences, overcome personal struggles and work together to stop the villain before the planet is destroyed.

Fill in the table below to practise applying C.R.I. to create an interesting problem in a story.

Challenge	**Key question:** What challenge does the Dream Team face? **Possible answer:** The Dream Team will need to stop ____________________ from ____________________________________ **Key question:** How does the problem force the Dream Team out of their comfort zone, to take action? **Possible answer:** The problem challenges the Dream Team by forcing them to ____ ____

Reactions	**Key question:** How does the Dream Team react emotionally and mentally when faced with this challenge? **Possible answer:** The Dream Team finds it difficult to ______________________ ______________________ because ______________________ ______________________ **Key question:** How do their reactions change as the story goes on? **Possible answer:** As the story goes on, the Dream Team learns to ______________________ ______________________
Impact	**Key question:** How does this problem affect the rest of the universe? i.e. What are the stakes of solving this problem? **Possible answer:** It affects the rest of the universe because ______________________ ______________________ If the Dream Team does not overcome this challenge, ______________________ ______________________ ______________________

Possible answers

Challenge	**Key question:** What challenge does the Dream Team face? **Possible answer:** The Dream Team will need to stop the dangerous villain from stealing the powerful artifact and destroying the planet. **Key question:** How does the problem force the Dream Team out of their comfort zone, to take action? **Possible answer:** The problem challenges the Dream Team by forcing them to work together despite their differences and personal struggles.
Reactions	**Key question:** How does the Dream Team react emotionally and mentally when faced with this challenge? **Possible answer:** The Dream Team finds it difficult to come up with a great plan because they have different ideas on the best way to stop the villain. **Key question:** How do their reactions change as the story goes on? **Possible answer:** As the story goes on, the Dream Team learns to set their differences aside and work together.
Impact	**Key question:** How does this problem affect the rest of the universe? i.e. What are the stakes of solving this problem? **Possible answer:** It affects the rest of the universe because the villain has evil intentions for stealing the powerful artifact. If the Dream Team does not overcome this challenge, people will get hurt and the planet will be destroyed. The dangerous villain could also harm others on other planets in the universe.

C.R.I.S.P. in Action!

Scenario

Bruno, a thirteen-year-old boy, finds himself stuck on a deserted island. He is forced to rely on himself to survive. Bruno is resourceful and intelligent but tends to give up easily. The island is full of surprises, both helpful and terrifying. What does Bruno encounter on the island? Does he manage to get off the island?

Fill in the table below to practise applying **C.R.I.** on your own to create an interesting problem in a story!

Challenge	**Key question:** What challenge does Bruno face? **Possible answer:** ______________________________ ______________________________ **Key question:** How does the problem force Bruno out of his comfort zone? What unforeseen surprises will Bruno encounter? **Possible answer:** ______________________________ ______________________________
Reactions	**Key question:** How does Bruno react emotionally and mentally when faced with this challenge? **Possible answer:** ______________________________ ______________________________ **Key question:** How do his feelings/thoughts/reactions change as the story goes on? **Possible answer:** ______________________________ ______________________________
Impact	**Key question:** How does this problem affect Bruno's future? What are the stakes of solving (or not solving) this problem? **Possible answer:** ______________________________ ______________________________ ______________________________ ______________________________ ______________________________

Possible answers

Challenge	**Key question:** What challenge does Bruno face? **Possible answer:** Bruno faces the challenge of surviving on the deserted island on his own and needs to find a way off the island to get back home. **Key question:** How does the problem force Bruno out of his comfort zone? What unforeseen surprises will Bruno encounter? **Possible answer:** Bruno is forced to rely on himself to survive. He encounters strange wild animals he never knew existed.
Reactions	**Key question:** How does Bruno react emotionally and mentally when faced with this challenge? **Possible answer:** Bruno starts off adjusting well to the challenge due to his resourcefulness and intelligence. He is curious about the things he encounters. However, he is also fearful as he doesn't know how to handle the strange wild animals. He gradually loses heart and thinks of giving up because his first plan to build a raft fails. **Key question:** How do his feelings/thoughts/reactions change as the story goes on? **Possible answer:** Bruno grows in perseverance as he learns not to give up easily.
Impact	**Key question:** How does this problem affect Bruno's future? What are the stakes of solving (or not solving) this problem? **Possible answer:** Bruno will be stuck on the island if he does not find a way to get off the island and return home safely. This would mean never seeing his friends or family ever again.

Puzzle Time 5

Across	Clue
1	Expect
5	Opposite of reject
6	Arrange
10	Appreciate

Down	Clue
2	Apply
3	Connect
4	Declare
7	Help
8	Apologise
9	Assume

Answers: Puzzle Time 5

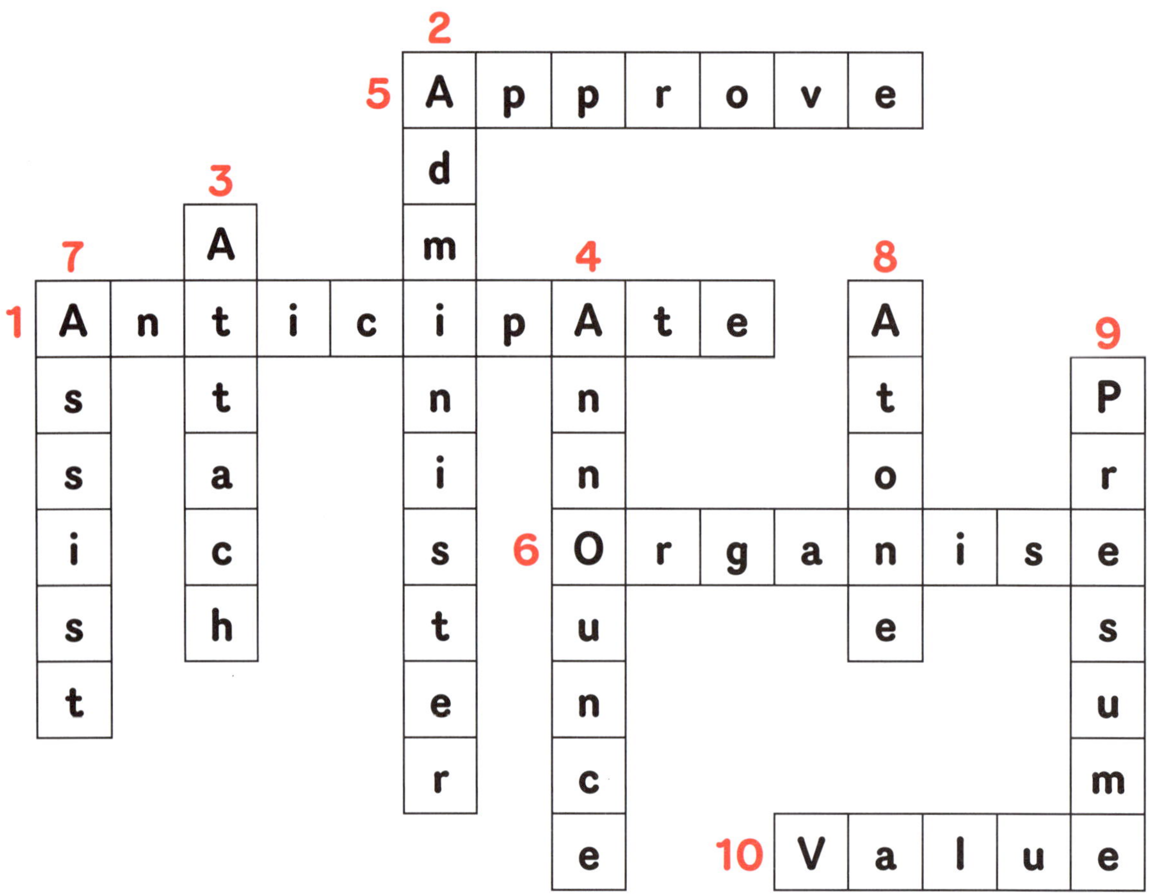

When problems rise, the heroes soar,
through battles fought and trials galore.
Their courage strong, as they find their way,
to bring light to every dark day.
The villain looms, the stakes rise high.
But through the storm, rings their battle cry.
With every fall, they'll rise again,
to break the chains that caused all pain.
In every heart, the answer lies,
a hero's will that never dies.
For every challenge that they face,
they'll find a way, a saving grace.

CHAPTER 6

Great Narratives

They've also overcome their own personal struggles, not just won the physical war. The solution has depth, because it solves both the internal and external problems.
That's it! It's that combination that makes the resolution feel satisfying. Readers want to see the character grow. They want to feel that the problem has left a mark, that it's changed the character in some way.
And in some stories, the solution doesn't completely fix everything, and that's okay too.
Through every page, the problem grows. The answers hidden in the prose. And when the final truth is shown, the journey leaves the hero grown.
That's a beautiful way to put it, Poppins! The journey is as important as the destination, if not more. When you're writing your own stories, think about how the problem shapes your characters. How does it challenge them? How does it force them to grow?
So in every great book, the problem isn't just a challenge for the character... it's what *makes* the character! When you craft your own stories, the problem is often what readers will remember most vividly. The problem and how the characters overcome it is the thing that sticks.
I think I understand. What starts out as one challenge can grow into something deeper as the story unfolds.
When you're writing, ask yourself:
How does the problem force my characters to grow? How does it challenge what they think they know? And how does the solution reflect that growth?
Oh, before I forget... my screenwriter friends like to say that the solution doesn't have to be easy. Sometimes, the best stories involve difficult choices. The solution the characters choose reflects their growth throughout the story.
The problem's twist, the hero's test, it pulls their strength from deep within their chest. The answer found is rarely neat, but it's the growth that makes it sweet.
The problems and resolutions are at the heart of the journey. It's what makes your readers care about the characters. It's what keeps your characters moving forward and discovering who they really are.

Key Concepts

In the previous chapter, we learned that the problem is a crucial part of every captivating story, as it helps to drive the plot forward. A well-crafted problem challenges the characters, pushing them to make decisions, overcome obstacles and ultimately grow.

Here, we will also explore how to craft a meaningful solution to the problem. The solution should not simply be a resolution of events. It is the journey towards solving the problem that makes it an interesting problem that captivates the reader.

The resolution can be a crucial moment of transformation, where we learn what the characters have learned about themselves, each other or the world. Often, characters will face failure in their first few attempts in solving the problem and overcoming the challenge. This is all part of the journey from problem to solution, which makes the solution meaningful and keeps the audience interested in the story.

Remember and apply **C.R.I.S.P.** to help you craft an interesting problem and meaningful solution in your story:

Challenge	Challenge your characters in ways that force them to make tough decisions. *How will this problem push the character out of their comfort zone?*
Reactions	Show the character's reactions (physical, emotional and mental). Don't allow them to solve the problem too quickly or you won't have a story. *How do they feel when faced with this challenge? Are they afraid, confused, determined etc.? Show how their internal strengths, weaknesses and struggles affect them as they face the problem.*
Impact	Make the problem matter. A strong problem affects not just the character but also their relationships, world or future. *How does solving (or failing to solve) the problem affect things? How do the stakes involved force the characters to act?*
Solution-finding	Show with vibrant descriptions how the characters devise a plan to tackle the problem, how they fail and how they try again. A good solution doesn't come easy. *How does the character's approach to solving the problem change as they fail and try again?*
Plan	Put your ideas all together in a mind map or a plan so that you can see how the problem and solution fit together. *How do the problem and solution fit together in the story?*

C.R.I.S.P. in Action!

Example:
Miguel is a boy wizard who has been enlisted by his wizarding school headmaster to collect three important items. It is a race against time, as an evil wizard is also trying to collect the three items, but for evil purposes. Miguel is bright and intelligent, but does not have confidence in himself to overcome the three trials of magic to collect the items and thwart the evil wizard's plans to have all the magical power in the world for himself.

See the table below as an example of how you can apply C.R.I.S.P. to create an interesting problem and meaningful solution in a story.

Challenge	**Key question:** What challenge does Miguel face? **Possible answer:** Miguel will need to figure out how to learn and perform the magic needed to get past the three magical trials in order to collect the three items. **Key question:** How does the problem force Miguel out of his comfort zone to take action? **Possible answer:** He faces the pressure from the evil wizard who is himself trying to collect the items for his evil plan
Reactions	**Key question:** How does Miguel react emotionally and mentally when faced with this challenge? **Possible answer:** He finds it difficult to master the magical skills and spells needed for the trials. This causes him to consider giving up and accepting that the evil wizard will succeed with his evil plan. **Key question:** How will his reactions change as the story goes on? **Possible answer:** As Miguel gradually learns the skills and magical spells, he gains more confidence in his ability. He is encouraged by his best friend, Sergio, who surprises Miguel by committing to joining him on the dangerous journey.
Impact	**Key question:** How does this problem affect the larger world? i.e. What are the stakes of solving this problem? **Possible answer:** It affects the wizarding world because the evil wizard is trying to take all the magical power in the world for himself.
Solution-finding	**Key question:** What is the first thing Miguel will do to try to overcome the challenge? Why does it fail? **Possible answer:** Miguel tries to face the first trial without any special training. He fails horribly because he is completely unprepared.

	Key question: How does Miguel re-strategise to try to overcome the challenge? **Possible answer:** Miguel asks his favourite professor for extra help and special training to ensure he will have all the magical skills he needs to overcome all three trials. **Key question:** How does Miguel succeed in the end? **Possible answer:** The special training helps Miguel overcome the first two trials. In the third trial, Sergio encourages Miguel and helps him to recall the right words for the finishing spell. At the end, Miguel sacrifices himself so that Sergio can finish off the evil wizard.
Plan	1. Miguel meets his wizarding school headmaster and is tasked with the quest to collect the three important items. 2. Miguel dives in and tries to complete the first trial without any help or special training. He fails. 3. Miguel feels the pressure of needing to complete the trials faster than the evil wizard. 4. Miguel asks for help from his favourite professor to ensure he is ready to attempt the trials again. 5. Miguel's best friend, Sergio, volunteers to help Miguel in his journey. 6. Miguel overcomes the first two trials successfully. 7. In the third trial, Miguel almost fails but eventually passes it with the help of Sergio. 8. Miguel fights the evil wizard. Miguel sacrifices himself, giving Sergio the chance to finish off the evil wizard.

C.R.I.S.P. in Action!

Scenario:
Antonio is a 12-year-old demigod boy living on an island. He just found out that his long-lost dad is actually the Greek god Zeus. Also, this news means that the monsters he has read about in Greek legends and myths are real! Antonio is a resourceful and capable boy, but is sometimes arrogant or overconfident. He is sent on a quest to find the lost Golden Fleece, which has powers to revive any dying or dead land, allowing it to grow crops again. All sorts of monsters try to stop Antonio from succeeding, as a crop-less island would be the perfect place for them to prey on the people. Antonio learns about the value of teamwork and how to be humble to receive help.

Fill in the table below to practise applying **C.R.I.S.P.** to create an interesting problem and meaningful solution in a story.

Challenge	**Key question:** What challenge does Antonio face? **Possible answer:** Antonio will need to find the ____________ to ____________ and stop ____________ ____________ **Key question:** How does the problem force Antonio out of his comfort zone, to take action? **Possible answer:** The problem challenges Antonio as it is too difficult for just ____________ ____________
Reactions	**Key question:** How does Antonio react emotionally and mentally when faced with this challenge? **Possible answer:** Zeus gives Antonio a special gift, ____________ This makes Antonio overconfident, and he ends up ____________ ____________ all on his own.

	Key question: How does his reaction change as the story goes on? **Possible answer:** As the story goes on, Antonio is forced to learn to be more ____ ____
Impact	**Key question:** How does this problem affect the larger world (more than just Antonio)? What are the stakes of solving this problem? **Possible answer:** It affects the larger world because the people on Antonio's island will ____ ____ if Antonio does not succeed.
Solution-finding	**Key question:** What is the first thing Antonio does to try to overcome the challenge? Why does it fail? **Possible answer:** Antonio tries to do it all by himself, but fails because ____ ____ ____ **Key question:** How does Antonio re-strategise to try to overcome the challenge? **Possible answer:** Antonio returns to his hometown. Upon reflection. he realises that he needs to be __________________________ and to ask for ____ ____. ______________________ step up to volunteer to help Antonio ____.

Plan	Give it a shot! Referring to the previous story example, use this space to plan the timeline of this story in point form.

Possible answers

Challenge	**Key question:** What challenge does Antonio face? **Possible answer:** Antonio will need to find the Golden Fleece to revive the land on his island and stop monsters from preying on his home village. **Key question:** How does the problem force Antonio out of his comfort zone, to take action? **Possible answer:** The problem challenges Antonio as it is too difficult for just Antonio to solve it on his own.
Reactions	**Key question:** How does Antonio react emotionally and mentally when faced with this challenge? **Possible answer:** Zeus gives Antonio a special gift, a golden sword. This makes Antonio overconfident, and he ends up trying to do it all on his own. **Key question:** How does his reaction change as the story goes on? **Possible answer:** As the story goes on, Antonio is forced to learn to be humbler and to accept help from others.
Impact	**Key question:** How does this problem affect the larger world (more than just Antonio)? What are the stakes of solving this problem? **Possible answer:** It affects the larger world because the people on Antonio's island will not be able to grow food and will be vulnerable to the monsters if Antonio does not succeed.
Solution-finding	**Key question:** What is the first thing Antonio does to overcome the challenge? Why does it fail? **Possible answer:** Antonio tries to do it all by himself, but fails because it is not possible for one person to sail such a boat on his own. There are too many things to manage, and Antonio loses track of them, causing him to fail. **Key question:** How does Antonio re-strategise to try to overcome the challenge? **Possible answer:** Antonio returns to his hometown. Upon reflection, he realises that he needs to be humble and ask for help from others. Two of Antonio's old schoolmates step up to volunteer to join Antonio on his quest to find the Golden Fleece.

Plan

Give it a shot! Referring to the previous story example, use this space to plan the timeline of this story in point form

1. The land on Antonio's island is becoming less and less fertile.
2. Antonio learns that his real dad is the Greek god Zeus.
3. He realises that this means the monsters he read about in the myths are real too.
4. Antonio is sent on a quest to find the Golden Fleece to revive his island.
5. Zeus gives him a golden sword to help him on his quest.
6. Antonio fails to get the boat to sail as he tries doing it all on his own.
7. Antonio learns to be humbler and to ask for help.
8. Two of Antonio's old schoolmates volunteer to join him.
9. Together, the three of them sail the seas and defeat the monsters.
10. They succeed in finding the Golden Fleece and bringing it home to their island.

C.R.I.S.P. in Action!

Scenario:
Carlos lives in a village below a tall mountain. Many people have tried to climb to the top of the mountain every year. In the process, some of them die due to the conditions at the top of the mountain. One day, our earth is in trouble! Due to radiation from the sun, many people have fallen sick. A team of three scientists have enlisted Carlos' help to guide them to the top of the mountain to retrieve a rare herb that can make people immune to the sun's radiation. Do Carlos and the team succeed? What obstacles do they face? How do they overcome them? What do they learn about themselves, each other, and the world in this journey to saving it?

Fill in the table below to practise applying C.R.I.S.P. to create an interesting problem and meaningful solution in a story!

Challenge	**Key question:** What challenges do Carlos and the scientists face? ____________________ ____________________ ____________________ ____________________ **Key question:** How does the problem force them out of their comfort zones? What unforeseen surprises do they encounter? ____________________ ____________________ ____________________ ____________________

Reactions	**Key question:** How do Carlos and the scientists react emotionally and mentally when faced with this challenge? __________ __________ __________ **Key question:** How do their feelings/thoughts/reactions change as the story goes on? __________ __________ __________
Impact	**Key question:** How does this problem affect the larger world? What are the stakes of solving (or not solving) this problem? __________ __________ __________ __________
Solution-finding	**Key question:** What is the first thing Carlos and the team will do to try to overcome the challenge? Why does it fail? __________ __________ __________ __________ **Key question:** How do they re-strategise to try to overcome the challenge? __________ __________ __________ __________

Plan	Use this space to plan the timeline of the story in point form.

Possible answers

Challenge	**Key question:** What challenges do Carlos and the scientists face? **Possible answer:** The people on Earth have fallen sick due to the sun's radiation. They need to find a cure. **Key question:** How does the problem force them out of their comfort zones? What unforeseen surprises do they encounter? **Possible answer:** The cure comes from a rare herb that lives only on the top of a tall mountain. Many people die trying to get the herb as they face terrible weather and climbing conditions during the journey.
Reactions	**Key question:** How do Carlos and the scientists react emotionally and mentally when faced with this challenge? **Possible answer:** Some of them lose heart and start to feel hopeless when trying to climb the mountain in terrible weather conditions. **Key question:** How do their feelings/thoughts/reactions change as the story goes on? **Possible answer:** Carlos encourages the team to keep going and not to give up. They share stories of their loved ones, which motivates them to accomplish their mission.
Impact	**Key question:** How does this problem affect the larger world? What are the stakes of solving (or not solving) this problem? **Possible answer:** People on Earth will fall sick and die if the herb is not retrieved and no cure is found.
Solution-finding	**Key question:** What is the first thing Carlos and the team will do to try to overcome the challenge? Why does it fail? **Possible answer:** They try to get to the herb by helicopter. This fails because of the terrible weather conditions. **Key question:** How do they re-strategise to try to overcome the challenge? **Possible answer:** They realise that they will need to climb the mountain the hard way, on foot.

Plan

Use this space to plan the timeline of the story in point form:

1. People on Earth fall sick from radiation.
2. Scientists figure out a rare herb found only at the top of a tall mountain can produce a cure.
3. They get the help of Carlos, who is a local of the village at the bottom of the mountain.
4. The first plan fails as the helicopter cannot fly in the terrible weather conditions.
5. The team and Carlos have to climb the mountain on foot.
6. They get discouraged.
7. Sharing the stories of their loved ones gives them fresh motivation to push on and accomplish their mission.
8. They eventually succeed after a tough climb to the top of the mountain.
9. The cure is made and people on Earth are saved.

Puzzle Time 6

Across	Clue
3	Opposite of separate
5	Evaluate
6	Cheer
9	Comfort
10	Challenge

Down	Clue
1	Change
2	Opposite of cooperate
4	Opposite of flee
7	Rejoice
8	Explain

Answers: Puzzle Time 6

											7			
					8						C			
				5	C	o	m	p	a	r	e			
		4			l						l			1
6	A	P	p	l	a	u	d	2			e			A
		u			r			C			b			l
		r			i	10	C	o	n	f	r	o	n	t
		s			f			m			a			e
		u			y			p			t			r
		e				3	M	e	r	g	e			
								t						
	9	C	o	n	s	o	l	e						

Across pages deep, the quest begins.
Chasing hopes and dreams, and a secret within.
Each character with strength to show,
in every tale, the seeds will grow.

The problems twist, the darkness falls,
but wisdom answers every call.
A path appears, the truth is clear,
in every heart, the way is near.

The story ends with lessons learned,
and broken hearts that are returned.
For in the end, through pain and strife,
we find the joy that shapes our life.

CHAPTER 7

What a Character!

Don, how do you think character arcs work in film?
Character arcs are crucial! A well-designed character should change over the course of a story. In *Finding Nemo*, Marlin starts off as overprotective and fearful. His journey across the ocean forces him to confront those fears and learn to trust others.
Alice, how do you think you could show this in writing?
Hmm... I could show it through describing the character's thoughts and feelings! Showing their internal struggles and growth will show the reader how the character has transformed, making their journey feel meaningful.
Exactly! Also, every character should have strengths and weaknesses. Flaws make them relatable, and strengths give them the ability to confront their challenges.
With every flaw, a chance to grow.
In every heart, a hidden glow.
A character's journey, a dance of fate,
where struggles shape, and dreams await.
Well summed up! What is one more thing we should consider in character design?
Hmm... a character's friends? Enemies?
Great! When you design a character, think about their relationships with others. How do they interact with friends, foes and mentors? Those dynamics can reveal a lot about who they are.
Oh! It's like the characters in *Harry Potter*. Harry's relationships with Ron and Hermione shape his journey. They bring out different sides of each other, and their interactions on their journey together illustrate how they grow together. How Harry interacts with Dumbledore and Voldemort also shows his maturity.
Exactly! Those relationships can also drive conflict and tension... which I see in film! Characters change in response to their interactions with others.
That's right! To elaborate, some ways you can capture this in writing is through dialogue and sharing the character's inner thoughts to create an engaging narrative. Through these things, characters influence each other to become better or worse.
So, as you develop your characters, remember to think about their design holistically.
Consider their appearance, backstory, relationships and how they evolve throughout the story.
Every aspect should work together to create a compelling and relatable character.
Let the characters' unique traits shine through!
Wonderful! They should feel real and vibrant, leaving a lasting impression on your readers.

Key Concepts

Great stories are driven by intriguing and memorable characters. They are the heart of the narrative and keep the reader engaged through their problems, choices and changes. Interesting characters draw readers in with their unique personalities, motivations and growth over time.

When a character faces challenges, their reactions, decisions and internal struggles create an intriguing mixture that makes learning about their story so much more interesting! This is because such internal struggles and growth draw emotional connections with the reader.

A well-crafted character has depth, making them feel real, relatable and complex. The way characters (heroes, villains or sidekicks) are designed shapes the entire story. This can be achieved through sharing or revealing their physical traits, dialogue, strengths and flaws.

Ultimately, an intriguing character makes a story more attractive to read and impactful for the reader, helping them to see the world through the character's eyes.

S.T.A.R.S.

Strengths and weaknesses	Strengths and weakness play an essential role in shaping a character. They heavily influence how a character is able to respond to others or to challenges they might face. What is the character's greatest strength? What are their biggest flaws or weaknesses? How do these strengths and weaknesses shape their actions?
Traits	A character's traits (their personality) are like their skeletal system. How a character's strengths, weaknesses, responses and other factors tie into a story depends heavily on their personality/character. What personality traits stand out the most in this character? Are they brave, kind, stubborn or quick-tempered? How do these traits affect how they interact with others?
Aspirations	A character's aspirations (their goals) are the things that matter most to the character. This gives the character something to pursue, adding depth to the story, instead of just existing. What does the character hope to achieve or become? What motivates them to pursue this goal? How do their aspirations drive the story forward?
Reactions to challenges	The way characters respond to the challenges they face in a story helps to determine what direction the story develops in. It is also crucial to how a character grows and develops (or not) over the course of a story. How does the character handle difficult situations? Do they face problems head-on or avoid them? How do these reactions shape their journey in the story?
Story impact	The strengths/weaknesses, personality, aspirations and reactions of a character affect other characters around them. This can have a big impact on a story. For example, it's understandable if a bully and his victim are not friendly with each other. However, imagine what it might do for the story if they somehow became friends later! This would provide a real twist in the story. *Note: It has to be believable!* How does the character influence the events of the story? How does the character's decisions impact other characters? By the end, how has the character changed and how has he/she changed the story?

S.T.A.R.S. in Action!

See the table below as an example of how you can apply S.T.A.R.S. to create an interesting problem and meaningful solution in a story.
Follow Don as he creates his own character!

Strengths and weaknesses	**Key question:** What is the character really good at? **Possible answer:** Leo is loyal to his friends and stands up for what's right. **Key question:** What are the character's biggest flaws? **Possible answer:** He is impulsive and rushes into action without thinking. **Key question:** How do these strengths and weaknesses shape his actions? **Possible answer:** His loyalty and courage drive him to stand up to his enemy, Tezrahan, but his impulsiveness often puts him and others in danger.
Traits	**Key question:** What personality traits stand out in this character? **Possible answer:** Leo is brave, determined and compassionate. **Key question:** How do these traits affect the character's interaction with others? **Possible answer:** His bravery inspires his friends to join him in fighting against evil, but his stubbornness sometimes creates conflict with them.
Aspirations	**Key question:** What does the character hope to achieve or become? **Possible answer:** Leo wants to defeat Tezrahan and bring peace to the world. **Key question:** What motivates him to pursue this goal? **Possible answer:** The death of his parents, caused by Tezrahan, motivates him to fight.
Reactions to challenges	**Key question:** How does the character handle difficult situations? **Possible answer:** Leo is courageous and confronts problems head-on, even when he's scared.
Story impact	**Key question:** How does the character influence the events of the story? **Possible answer:** Leo's decisions lead to major turning points, like destroying Tezrahan's machine, despite the temptation of using it for his own selfish needs to bring his parents back from the dead. **Key question:** By the end of the story, how has the character changed? **Possible answer:** By the end, Leo matures, realising the importance of sacrifice and the strength found in unity with others.

S.T.A.R.S. in Action!

Fill in the table below to use **S.T.A.R.S.** to create an interesting character!

Refer to the following paragraph for more information on the character:

> *Aria Brightwood is a gifted young girl living in the magical world of Lanzarus. With a talent for elemental magic, she excels at manipulating fire and water, which helps her to defend her village from a variety of threats. However, Aria is not the most confident person. She finds it challenging to trust her skills, especially when faced with powerful enemies. Her curious nature drives her to seek knowledge and become a great protector. She is motivated by her desire to protect her loved ones and prove her worth. Throughout her journey, Aria learns to confront her fears head-on. She discovers that true strength comes not just from her magical abilities, but from her resilience and the friendships she forges along the way. By the end of her story, she emerges as a confident leader, ready to guide others in their battles against dark forces threatening Lanzarus.*

Strengths and weaknesses	**Key question:** What is the character really good at? Aria is excellent at ______________________ ______________________ **Key question:** What are the character's biggest flaws? She struggles with ______________________ ______________________ **Key question:** How do these strengths and weaknesses shape her actions in the story? Her talent in ______________________ helps her to ______________________. Her weakness is ______________________ ______________________ makes it difficult for her to ______________________.
Traits	**Key question:** What personality traits stand out the most in this character? Aria is ____________, ____________ and ______________________ **Key question:** How do these traits affect how the character interacts with others? As Aria is ______________________, she tends to ______________________. This leads to ______________________.

Aspirations	**Key question:** What does the character hope to achieve or become? Aria wants to ______________________________ because ______________________________. **Key question:** What motivates her to pursue this goal? She is motivated by ______________________________ especially when ______________________________ ______________________________.
Reactions to challenges	**Key question:** How does the character handle difficult situations? When faced with challenges, Aria tends to ______________________________ ______________________________. **Key question:** Does she face problems head-on or avoid them? Aria usually ______________________________ her problems, which results in ______________________________.
Story impact	**Key question:** How does the character influence the events in the story? Aria influences the story by ______________________________ ______________________________ **Key question:** By the end, how has the character changed? By the end of the story, Aria has ______________________________ ______________________________ because of ______________________________. This shows that ______________________________ ______________________________.

Possible answers

Strengths and weaknesses	**Key question:** What is the character really good at? **Possible answer:** Aria is excellent at elemental magic, controlling fire and water. **Key question:** What are the character's biggest flaws? **Possible answer:** She struggles with self-confidence. **Key question:** How do these strengths and weaknesses shape her actions in the story? **Possible answer:** Her talent in elemental magic helps her to defend her village from different monster threats. Her weakness is her lack of self-confidence which makes it difficult for her to trust her skills in defeating powerful enemies.
Traits	**Key question:** What personality traits stand out the most in this character? **Possible answer:** Aria is curious, loving and fiercely desires to protect her loved ones. **Key question:** How do these traits affect how the character interacts with others? **Possible answer:** As Aria is not self-confident, she tends to be nervous and panics when faced with difficulty. This leads to her learning to be more confident and resilient through the friendships she makes along the way.
Aspirations	**Key question:** What does the character hope to achieve or become? **Possible answer:** Aria wants to protect her village because dark forces are threatening Lanzarus. **Key question:** What motivates her to pursue this goal? **Possible answer:** She is motivated by her love for her village, especially when she faces difficulty.
Reactions to challenges	**Key question:** How does the character handle difficult situations? **Possible answer:** When faced with challenges, Aria tends to get nervous and give up if the problem is not overcome easily. **Key question:** Does she face problems head-on or avoid them? **Possible answer:** Aria usually avoids her problems, which results in the problem not being solved.
Story impact	**Key question:** How does the character influence the events in the story? **Possible answer:** Aria influences the story by growing in resilience and becoming more able to protect Lanzarus. **Key question:** By the end, how has the character changed? **Possible answer:** By the end of the story, Aria becomes a confident leader and protector of Lanzarus, because she is forced to grow in resilience and confidence. This shows that it is how one chooses to respond to difficulty that determines how one grows.

S.T.A.R.S. in Action!

Fill in the table below to practise applying **S.T.A.R.S.** to create an interesting character!

Strengths and weaknesses	What is the character really good at? __________ __________ What are the character's biggest flaws or weaknesses? __________ __________ How do these strengths and weaknesses shape their actions in the story? __________ __________ __________ __________
Traits	What personality traits stand out the most in this character? __________ __________ How do these traits affect how the character interacts with others? __________ __________ __________ __________
Aspirations	What does the character hope to achieve or become? __________ __________ What motivates him/her to pursue this goal? __________ __________ __________

Reactions to challenges	How does the character handle difficult situations? __________ __________ Does he/she face problems head-on or avoid them? __________ __________
Story impact	How does the character influence the events of the story? __________ __________ __________ __________ By the end, how has the character changed? __________ __________ __________ __________

In the space below, use the details that you have listed in the S.T.A.R.S. table above to write a short paragraph describing your new character!

Puzzle Time 7

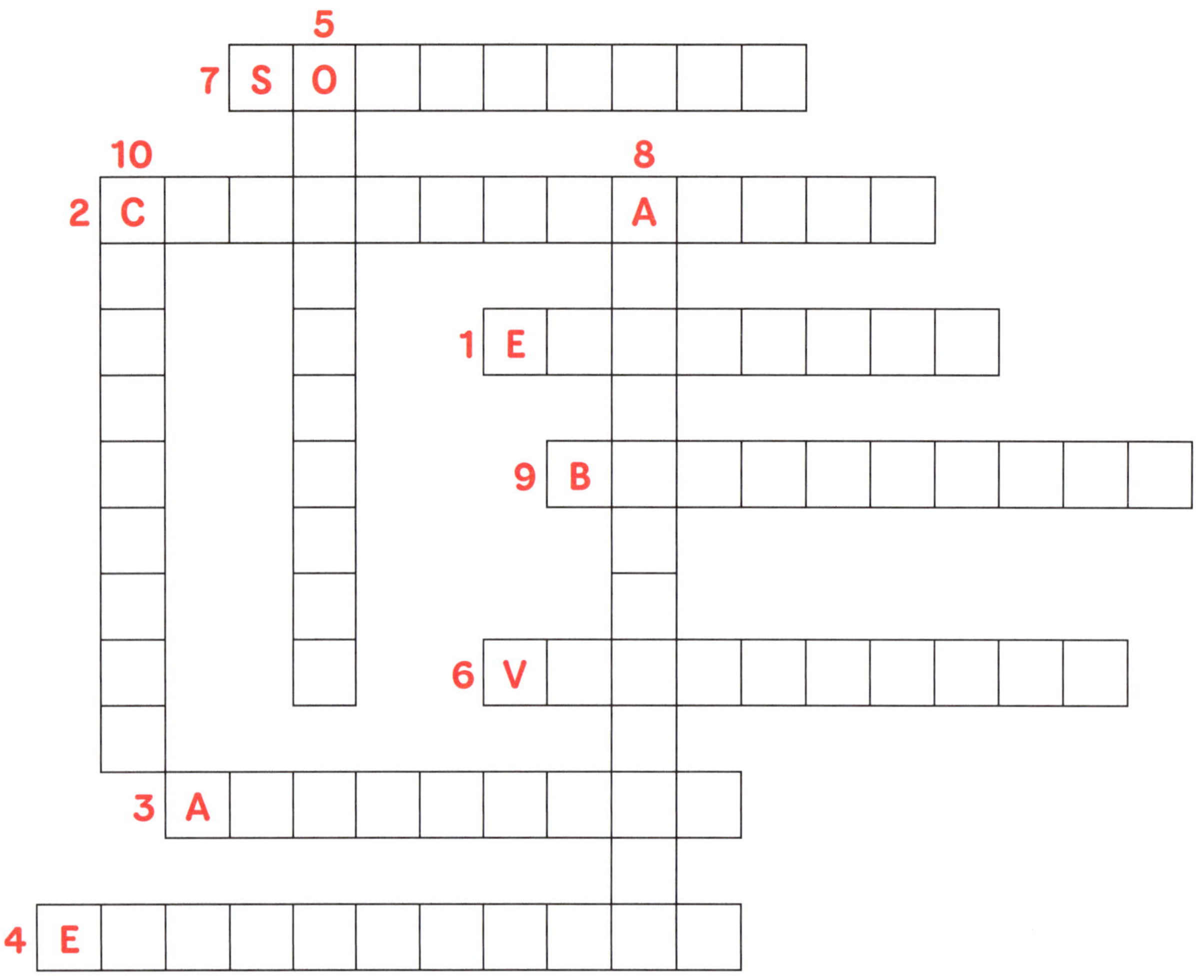

Across	Clue
1	Elated
2	Thoughtful
3	Indifferent
4	Frustrated
6	Spiteful
7	Opposite of jubilant
9	Opposite of understanding

Down	Clue
5	Hopeful
8	Fearful
10	Opposite of indifferent

Answers: Puzzle Time 7

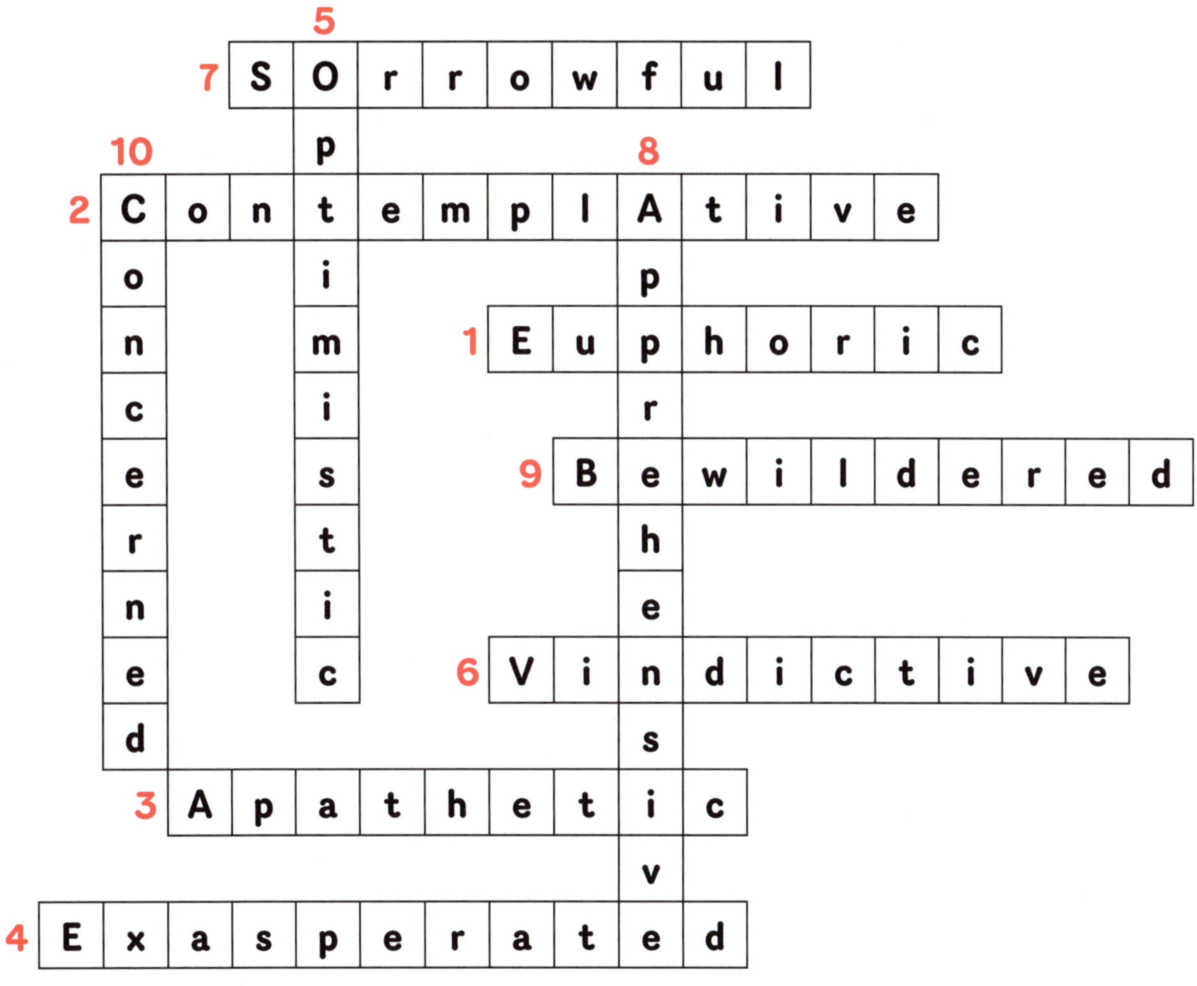

Creating characters brave and bright,
with traits that shine whether day and night.
Their dreams and fears, their highs and lows,
are what make stories truly grow.

Each flaw, each strength, each little quirk,
gives them life and makes stories work.
They leap from pages, as real as air,
and leave us moved, beyond compare.

So, craft them with care, and let them lead.
For in their steps, the tale will breed,
a world of wonders, deep and wide,
where readers journey by their side.

CHAPTER 8

It was a Dark and Stormy Paragraph

Haha! Good one, Don! If you could all create a setting for this class to be more exciting, what would you do?
I would decorate this entire place with beautiful plants and flowers to make us feel like we are outdoors in a beautiful garden.
I would have shelves and shelves of books ranging from the classics to modern day works of fiction. All to inspire me to write great stories. After all, we are trying to create the best setting to learn to write!
That sounds boring...
What would you do, Don? How would you change this classroom to create a setting that you think is most conducive for you to learn in?
I was thinking of creating a cosy setting with sofas, games and a snack corner... but, I think that might make me lazy and the games would definitely distract me.
Hmm... are you thinking what I am thinking?
That this is perhaps the best setting for one to learn in because there are no distractions?
Haha! Sounds like you have all understood the importance of creating a setting!

Key Concepts

The key in creating a setting is to Show, not Tell. This technique is essential in creating an immersive experience for the reader as they envision what is being described in your story.

<table>
<tr><th>Key Aspects</th><th>Tell</th><th>Show</th><th>Outcome</th></tr>
<tr><td>Atmosphere — Taste</td><td>The air was salty.</td><td>The taste of salt tickled her throat as she inhaled deeply.</td><td rowspan="7">There were only 20 families that lived in the village away from the hustle and bustle of the city just a short ferry ride away.

Wooden houses raised on stilts lined the shore.

The sun, a glowing orange orb, peeked its head just above the horizon, brightening the ocean from a dark blue to a beautiful turquoise revealing the life beneath the ocean.

The taste of salt tickled her throat as she inhaled deeply.

The warm sea breeze washed away all the tension she had been carrying in her shoulders.

Samantha took a deep breath and smiled as she looked across at the village below.

Everything looked so small from the balcony protruding high up at the very top of the lighthouse.

Fishermen floated to shore on their wooden rowboats carrying heavy nets swollen with their catch of the day. It was the biggest catch they had gotten all month, and everyone was excited.

Samantha was excited too, but for different reasons. It was an important day for her because she was finally going to tell her family the big news.</td></tr>
<tr><td>Atmosphere — Touch</td><td>It was windy.</td><td>The warm sea breeze washed away all the tension she had been carrying in her shoulders.</td></tr>
<tr><td>Atmosphere — Time and place</td><td>It was sunrise.</td><td>The sun, a glowing orange orb, peeked its head just above the horizon, brightening the ocean from a dark blue to a beautiful turquoise, revealing the life beneath the ocean.</td></tr>
<tr><td>Atmosphere — Sound</td><td>The waves were strong.</td><td>Waves crashed loudly onto the rocks below the lighthouse.</td></tr>
<tr><td>Atmosphere — Sight</td><td>It was a bird's eye view of the ocean.</td><td>Everything looked so small from the balcony protruding high up at the very top of the lighthouse.</td></tr>
<tr><td>Symbolism and cultural context</td><td>It was a quiet fishing village in the 1950s</td><td>There were only 20 families that lived in this village, away from the hustle and bustle of the city just a short ferry ride away.

Wooden houses raised on stilts lined the shore. Fishermen floated to shore on their wooden rowboats carrying heavy nets swollen with their catch of the day.</td></tr>
<tr><td>Foreshadowing</td><td>Something was going to happen.</td><td>Samantha took a deep breath and smiled as she looked at the village below.

Samantha was excited too, but for different reasons. It was an important day for her because she was finally going to tell her family the big news.</td></tr>
</table>

Key Concepts

Remember these essential **F.A.C.T.S.** when creating a setting in your story!

F - Foreshadowing

These are elements that hint at future events. They enhance the reading experience and create anticipation.

A - Atmosphere and Mood

The aspects that contribute to the overall sense of the story. The narration will engage the reader emotionally. For example, a gloomy and cloudy setting might create the feeling of tension or sadness, while a bright and vibrant landscape could instil a sense of joy.

C - Cultural Context

This shapes cultural elements. It tells us what background/culture the characters come from. It can even reveal the influence their society has on their beliefs and actions.

T - Time and Place

This tells us where and when the story takes place. It establishes the background in the story and has an effect on the characters' social norms and behaviours.

S - Symbolism

Symbolism plays a role in representing broader concepts. For example, a community within a busy city or isolation within a desert.

Some Examples!

Sports Day

The stadium pulsed with the energy of students cheering for their teams. Alice and Poppins squeezed past a group of overenthusiastic cheerleaders, carefully balancing their snacks and drinks in both hands. Don somehow found a quiet corner on the bleachers where he could observe everything and take notes for his next screenplay. "The races are about to begin!" Coach's voice boomed through the speakers. Sports Day had officially begun.

School Begins

The classroom buzzed with anticipation. Sunlight filtered through the dusty windows, illuminating desks strewn with clean fresh textbooks and stationery. Don sat with his arms folded, observing his fellow classmates update one another about their summer vacations, as if he were watching a play in a theatre. Poppins whispered excitedly to Alice, who was busy arranging her coloured pens. It was the unmistakeable scene of the first day of school.

Finding the Movie

The living room was a cosy haven filled with comfortable, plush furniture. A faint scent of cookies baking in the oven wafted from the kitchen as Poppins plopped onto the couch next to Don. "No, not this one," said Don dryly. "It's not a good movie," he declared. Alice rolled her eyes as she switched movie titles on the screen for what felt like the hundredth time. "The cookies will be done by the time we decide on which movie to watch," Poppins said sarcastically, as she gave Alice a sly wink.

Activities

1. Set the Stage

Create your own scene set in a location of your choice. In one paragraph, describe the setting using only sensory details — sight, smell, touch, taste, sound — and actions that will allow your reader to envision the scene and feel the atmosphere and mood.

____

____

____

2. Match the Stage

City from the Future	The Magic Forest	Busy Flea Market	Abandoned Playground	Cosy Cabin in the Mountains

Here are some settings in the table above. Match them with the stories on the left column below. An example has been provided below for you.

Story	Which setting does the story describe?
After relocating to an old town, two siblings find an old playground that is overgrown with trees and plants. Amidst the foliage, they find a treasure map. They follow the clues that lead them to discover the mystery of the playground's abandonment and what happened to the children who used to play there.	
Street vendors and vibrant colours line the most popular shopping district in Singapore. Everything from clothes to kitchenware are sold at a bargain attracting people of all generations. When a housewife buys a new oil lamp, she realises it is magic and quickly learns the meaning of 'be careful what you wish for'.	
In the middle of the night, under giant neon digital billboards amongst towering skyscrapers, hoverboards and flying cars, an angry young man who just lost his job as an Artificial Intelligence Designer hacks into his company's central system to destroy all possibility of weaponising human droids.	
Five best friends go on a Christmas vacation in a remote cabin in the Swiss Alps. They stumble upon an old diary with an eerie and horrifying history about the cabin. Over the next week, friendships are put to the test as this close group of friends experience strange happenings around the house.	
Where leaves of giant trees glow in the night and mushrooms hum beautiful melodies, two mystical squirrel-like creatures with wings emerge out of their tree homes awakened by the unfamiliar sound of human footsteps.	

3. Transform the Stage!

Read the paragraph below and rewrite the story by changing the setting. In doing so, describe how the new setting changes the characters' actions and the overall story.

On an island tucked away in the Gulf of Thailand, a quiet village is nestled between the valley of steep hills and the still waters of the South China Sea. The fiery sun is just waking up, slowly but surely painting the sky hues of light orange and blue. Young Tutu and Minta stir in their beds, tucking themselves deeper under the covers. It is the first day of school for the children. But for the cows that live in the valleys, it is just another day of grazing the open grass fields. "You can get on," Mai tells her daughter and son, as she steadies her dusty but very trusty scooter. Tutu's eyes brighten as he feels the vibrations of the scooter starting. Minta holds her younger brother tighter and throws her free hand in the air, feeling the wind as Mai snakes through the bumpy, sandy pathway leading them away from the comfort of their little village and towards the start of yet another adventurous year in school.

4. Describe your Stage!

Describe a setting for your story using the images on the left as a guide.

	E.g., Bright white marshmallow clouds covered the sky as little crystals of water droplets floated gently down onto the street, each one unique and a marvel of nature.

5. Create Your Stage

Pick two of the four images below as inspiration to write your own story. Remember to describe your setting in as much detail as possible.

A

B

C

D

Puzzle Time 8

Across	Clue
3	Ignore
5	Dim
8	Expect
9	Empathetic

Down	Clue
1	Assess
2	Brighten
4	Opposite of exhaust
6	Opposite of administer
7	Opposite of rejuvenate
10	Hot

Answers: Puzzle Time 8

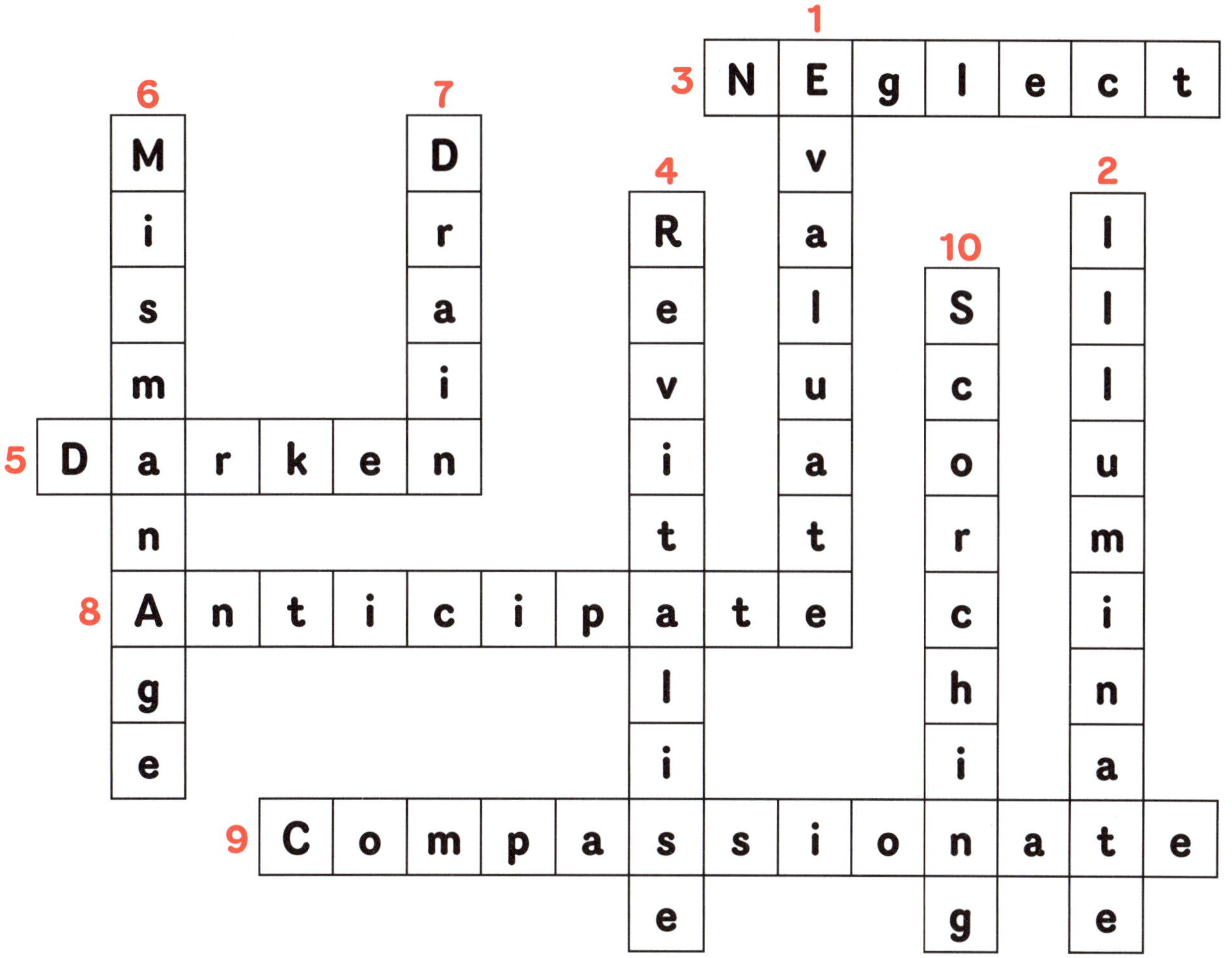

To tell a good story,
you've got to put on a show.
Is it in a town or a forest?
Is it dull or does it glow?

Take us on an adventure,
With wonders to find.
Your settings can light up the mind,
sparking imagination of every kind!

CHAPTER 9

Words, Words, Words

Good! How would you describe the intensity of a fight?
I could talk about their expressions — their faces were red with anger, and their actions — they raised their fists preparing for a fight.
That's very good, Alice!
Words bring my imagination to life, they can make any scene come so alive!
There she goes again!
She's right though. I think that describing a scene really brings what I imagine to life.
Yes, I suppose that is true. When I'm directing a scene, for the actors to envision what I am envisioning, I need to describe everything in as much detail as possible.
Well done, everyone! Now, shall we put all this into action and do some activities to help us improve our descriptive skills?
Yes!

Key Concepts

Key Aspects	Tell	Show
Build Atmosphere	It was a sunny day.	Sunlight shone through the leaves, creating thin rays of light on the freshly cut green grass. It was as if the sun was stretching its arms as it rose from a deep slumber.
Create Vivid Imagery	The park was nice.	Leaves of green, red, yellow and orange crowned the towering trees in the park. The first colours of autumn brought vibrance and colour much to everyone's delight.
Enhance Emotional Impact	He was happy.	He leapt out of his seat in joy and threw his hands in the air.
Develop Character	She was upset.	Her face grew red as she felt the heat rise from her chest to her ears. She clenched her fists in an effort to hold back from lashing out at her brother.
Increase Engagement	They walked into the house.	They crept quietly into the dark empty house. They could feel the hairs on the back of their necks beginning to stand as they passed the eerie hallway.
Strengthen the Narrative	There was a war.	Amidst the rubble where skyscrapers once stood, fighter jets roared overhead and tanks rolled through the streets threateningly as civilians rushed back into their homes to seek shelter.
Encourage Imagination	The palace was big.	The royal palace stood in all its grandeur amidst the townhouses. Its sprawling gardens were filled with flowers of every colour and ornate fountains, infusing the palace grounds with serenity and beauty.

Key Concepts

I.C.E. - T

I - Imagery
Inviting a reader to imagine every setting and scene is a valuable aspect that sparks creativity in the reader and helps them to envision the story with greater clarity.

C - Character Development
As a story evolves, so should the characters of the story. Describing their character unveils traits and motivations.

E - Engage Emotions
Describing the characters' emotions will allow the reader to feel what the character is feeling. It helps them relate or empathise with the characters.

T - Tension
Tension creates suspense and enhances the stakes of the narrative.

Some Examples!

Let's Go to the Movies

Brightly lit posters showcased the movies being screened outside the cinema. As they approached the cinema, Tim and Nelly's excitement grew.

"Wow! *Spider-Man: Homecoming* has such an awesome poster!" Tim exclaimed, barely able to contain his joy. It had been a busy week of studying, and the smell of fresh popcorn and plush red seats could not be better. Nelly had already made a beeline for his favourite blend of buttered and caramel popcorn, while Tim ran over to the ticket booth to collect their tickets. It was a good thing Tim had already booked them online, so they did not have to stand in the long queue.

Dinosaurs at the Science Centre

Giant statues of dinosaurs lined the doorway of the massive Science Centre. The Dinosaur Exhibition was in town and both children and adults were excited to see replicas of these extinct giants. The air was electric with curiosity as crowds gathered around the exhibits, taking photos and learning about the history of dinosaurs and each of their unique qualities. Though there was a myriad of other exhibitions, experiments and displays to experience, the Dinosaur Exhibition was the star of the Science Centre that day.

School's Out!

The last bell of the term was music to the ears of all students of Palmtree Primary. Children ran out of their classrooms, gleefully laughing and cheering on their way to the school's main gate. Many of their parents were waiting for them with open arms and the promise of fun vacations in the coming weeks. Amidst the bustle of excited school children, a little boy sat quietly in the school canteen looking down at his shoes.

"What's the matter, Luke? Aren't you glad our school holidays have begun?" asked his best friend, Howie.

"Not really. Both my parents have to go away on a business trip. There's no one at home," Luke said while looking down at his shoes, trying to hide the tears threatening to fall.

"Well!" exclaimed Howie. "That means it's going to be a vacation of sleepovers, camping in our backyard and slumber parties! We're going to plan it all at my place. Come on, let's go!" Howie said excitedly.

A smile slowly spread across Luke's face. He really did have the best friend in the world.

Activities

1. Descriptive snaps!

In one paragraph, describe your favourite place in as much detail as possible. Your reader should be able to see, feel and sense every aspect of this place vividly.

2. Plain and exciting scenes

Improve the plain settings in the left column and create an exciting paragraph of your own!

Plain	Exciting
It was a rainy day.	*E.g., Dark clouds covered the sky completely and suddenly, rain began to pour incessantly as if someone had turned on the faucet at full blast.*
It was a crowded day at the fun fair.	
The stadium was empty.	
The birthday party was fun.	
It was a sunny day at the beach.	
School was fun.	

3. Setting Emotions in Motion

Select one of the emotions expressed in the images below. Using descriptive writing skills, write a scene that describes the emotion you have selected.

4. Picture postcard

Imagine that you are on your dream vacation writing a postcard to your best friend. How would you describe the place that you are in, the people that you have met, the food you have eaten and the sights that you have seen? Use the space below to write your postcard.

Puzzle Time 9

Across	Clue
3	Opposite of gentle
5	Opposite of recover
7	Suggest
8	Need
9	Settle

Down	Clue
1	Reorganise
2	To look like
4	Recognise
6	Regret
10	Bright

Answers: Puzzle Time 9

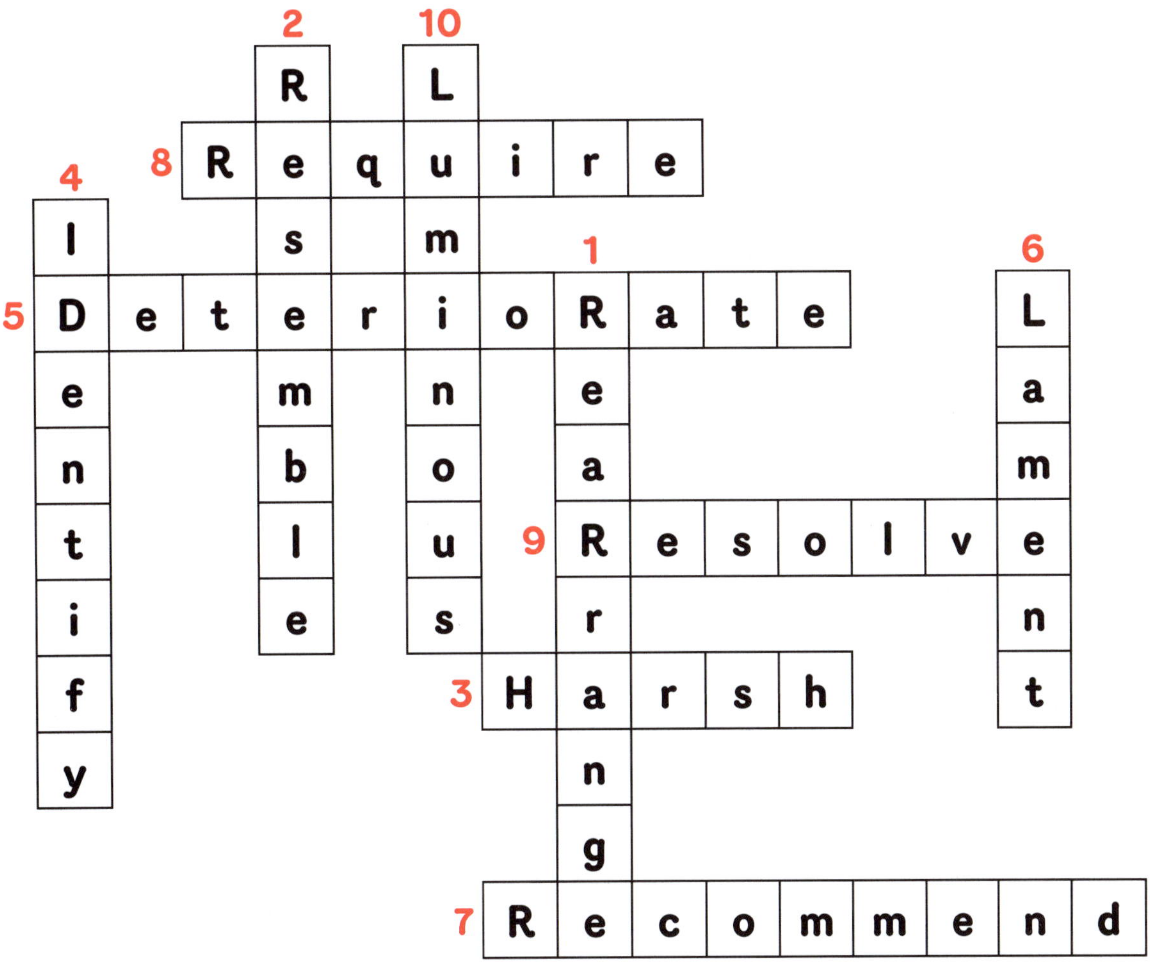

In all stories, you must set a stage.
Is it in a quiet garden or a boxing ring?
Vivid descriptions will give us an idea.
Let your imagination sing!

It could be the scent of fresh roses,
or the rumble of a train.
Sights, sounds, smells, even textures,
can depict scenes of joy or pain!

CHAPTER 10

Punctuation and Sentence Boundaries

What else is punctuation good for? I'll give you another clue. It can combine two words into one. And Alice just used it.
Did I? I don't think I did. What'd I say?
She did it again — twice! Who can tell?
I know! She collapsed 'do not' into 'don't'!
And 'what did' into 'what'd'!
Well done, Don and Poppins! Now, just as it is with all things, we can also overdo it with punctuation. Can anyone give me an example of such a situation?
With exclamation marks and question marks! Whenever Alice writes, she likes to emphasise a statement with multiple exclamation marks.
I do not!!!!!
If the words you just said could be seen, they would've had five exclamation marks after it.
Whoops, I guess I do get carried away?
I think my favourite punctuation mark is the apostrophe.
Why's that?
Because it combines two words into one, so I can write less!
Sounds like you've all understood the importance of punctuation. Now let's put it to the test!

Key Concepts

Key Aspects	Tell	Show
Period (.)	Indicates the end of a sentence	Poppins says that she wants three dogs.
Comma (,)	Separates nouns or phrases	She is going to call them Jack, Jill and Jim.
Apostrophe (')	Indicates a contraction or possession	"Isn't she going to ask her mother first?" asked Alice. "Why doesn't she just play with her neighbour's dog?"
Quotation marks (")	Encloses direct quotations or speech	Don exclaimed, "No way! It might bite her."
Question mark (?)	Indicates a question	"Is it fierce?" asked Alice.
Exclamation mark (!)	Expresses emphasis on a statement or a strong emotion	"It's the fiercest dog in the neighbourhood!" exclaimed Don.
Dash (—)	Indicates a break in thought or adds emphasis to a statement	She says there is a discount right now — a huge discount.
Semicolon (;)	Connects independent but closely related statements	She should not buy dogs on a whim; they aren't toys.
Colon (:)	Introduces a list, explanation or quote	"My mother says that I can get the dogs! I have three colours to choose from: pink, blue and orange!" said Poppins.
Ellipsis (...)	Indicates a thought that is trailing off or an unfinished sentence	"Oh, she's not talking about real dogs, Don..." smiled Alice.
Interrobang (‽)	Combines an exclamation mark and a question mark. It is an expression of both excitement and disbelief at the same time	"For a moment, we thought she was going to get pink, blue and orange dogs‽" laughed Don.

Punctuation seems like a very simple aspect of writing. It is! Yet, it has the power to inject drama into a story. It can excite readers quickly! It can help us ask questions, can't it? It can instil doubt... and it can help you to express your thoughts with clarity, structure and detail. Here's an example:

Without punctuation	With punctuation
Paul Alex and Dan walked into the studio Mrs Lee raised an eyebrow at how casually they walked in as if they did not know the whole class was waiting for them Mrs Lee suddenly sprung from her seat and clapped loudly here come the royal prince and princesses she declared with a glint in her eye the class erupted in laughter and started clapping along with her Paul Alex and Dan bowed their heads in embarrassment as they walked to their seats	Paul, Alex and Dan walked into the studio. Mrs Lee raised an eyebrow at how casually they walked in, as if they did not know the whole class was waiting for them. Mrs Lee suddenly sprung from her seat and clapped loudly. "Here come the royal princes!" she declared with a glint in her eye. The class erupted in laughter and started clapping along with her. Paul, Alex and Dan bowed their heads in embarrassment as they walked to their seats.

Food for Thought...

Were you able to see the difference in the two paragraphs? How did reading either one make you feel? Was it easy reading the paragraph without punctuation? Did the paragraph with punctuation allow you to paint the scene with more clarity?

Now let's put everything we have learned to practice!

Activities

1. Compare the dots and lines

Compare the two passages below and identify punctuation mistakes in one of them.

Passage 1a
In the small town of Timothy's Creek, Don, Alice, Poppins and their friends were buzzing with excitement for the annual town carnival. "Last one to the Ferris wheel is a rotten egg!" Don yelled. Everyone was running towards the Ferris wheel when a scream suddenly pierced the air. Everyone stopped dead in their tracks and looked around. "Guys, where's Pete?" Poppins broke the silence.

Passage 1b
In the small town of Timothy's Creek. Don; Alice; Poppins and their friends were buzzing with excitement for the annual town carnival. "Last one to the Ferris wheel is a rotten egg?' Don yelled. Everyone was running towards the Ferris wheel when a scream suddenly pierced the air; everyone stopped dead in their tracks and looked around! "Guys, where's Pete?" Poppins broke the silence

2. Spot the Mistakes

Spot the mistakes in the following passages.

Passage 2
Alice, Don, Poppins and their friends split up to search the carnival grounds. Don checked the Haunted House while Alice checked the House of Mirrors... Poppins looked around at the game booths. Did you see Pete? Don asked when everyone gathered back at the meeting point. Why'd you let him out of your sight? asked Poppins while looking at Sarah. I asked you to look after him while I got the ice cream! Yes well, you shouldn't have left him in the first place if you were such a good sister, Sarah retorted defensively.

Passage 3

"Ladies; let's not argue. We need to find Pete before it gets dark;" said Don. Let's continue searching and regroup here again in 20 minutes: After 10 minutes of looking around the Ferris wheel. Sarah suddenly grabbed Alice: "Look! That's Pete's cap!" Alice whipped around and saw Pete's unmistakable neon green cap... being worn by someone else! "No way. Who's that wearing Pete's cap?" Alice asked. "I don't know but we have to follow him;" yelled Sarah. "Come on!"

Passage 4

"Hey! Hey you!" Don shouted. A boy wearing a neon green cap turned around. "Yes? he asked. "Where'd you get this cap from?" Don demanded, reaching out to grab it. "Hey, watch it!:" said the young boy. I got it as a gift from some guy: "Where's this guy?" asked Poppins. "Hes' right here," came a voice from behind Poppins. "Pete! Where have you been this whole time? we"re all worried sick about you!"

"I had followed you to the ice-cream stand! Didn"t you see me? I knelt to tie my shoelaces and when I stood up; you were gone."

"How do you explain this guy here wearing your cap then?"

"Well; I told him he could have it if he could help me find my sister and friends. And it worked!" Pete beamed.

"Oh Pete!" Poppins groaned. "You"re going to give me a heart attack one day?

Answers for Passages 2-4

Passage 2

Alice, Don, Poppins and their friends split up to search the carnival grounds. Don checked the Haunted House while Alice checked the House of Mirrors. Poppins looked around at the game booths. "Did you see Pete?" Don asked, when everyone gathered back at the meeting point.
"Why'd you let him out of your sight?" asked Poppins while looking at Sarah. "I asked you to look after him while I got the ice cream!"
"Yes, well, you shouldn't have left him in the first place if you were such a good sister!" Sarah retorted defensively.

Passage 3

"Ladies, let's not argue. We need to find Pete before it gets dark," said Don. "Let's continue searching and regroup here again in 20 minutes." After 10 minutes of looking around the Ferris wheel, Sarah suddenly grabbed Alice, "Look! That's Pete's cap!" Alice whipped around and saw Pete's unmistakable neon green cap... being worn by someone else! "No way. Who's that wearing Pete's cap?" Alice asked. "I don't know but we have to follow him!" yelled Sarah. "Come on!"

Passage 4

"Hey! Hey you!" Don shouted. A boy wearing a neon green cap turned around. "Yes?" he asked.
"Where'd you get this cap from?" Don demanded, reaching out to grab it. "Hey, watch it!" said the young boy. "I got it as a gift from some guy."
"Where's this guy?" asked Poppins.
"He's right here," came a voice from behind Poppins.
"Pete! Where have you been this whole time? We were all worried sick about you!"
"I had followed you to the ice-cream stand! Didn't you see me? I knelt to tie my shoelaces and when I stood up, you were gone."
"How do you explain this guy here wearing your cap then?"
"Well, I told him he could have it if he could help me find my sister and friends. And it worked!" Pete beamed.
"Oh Pete!" Poppins groaned. "You're going to give me a heart attack one day!"

Puzzle Time 10

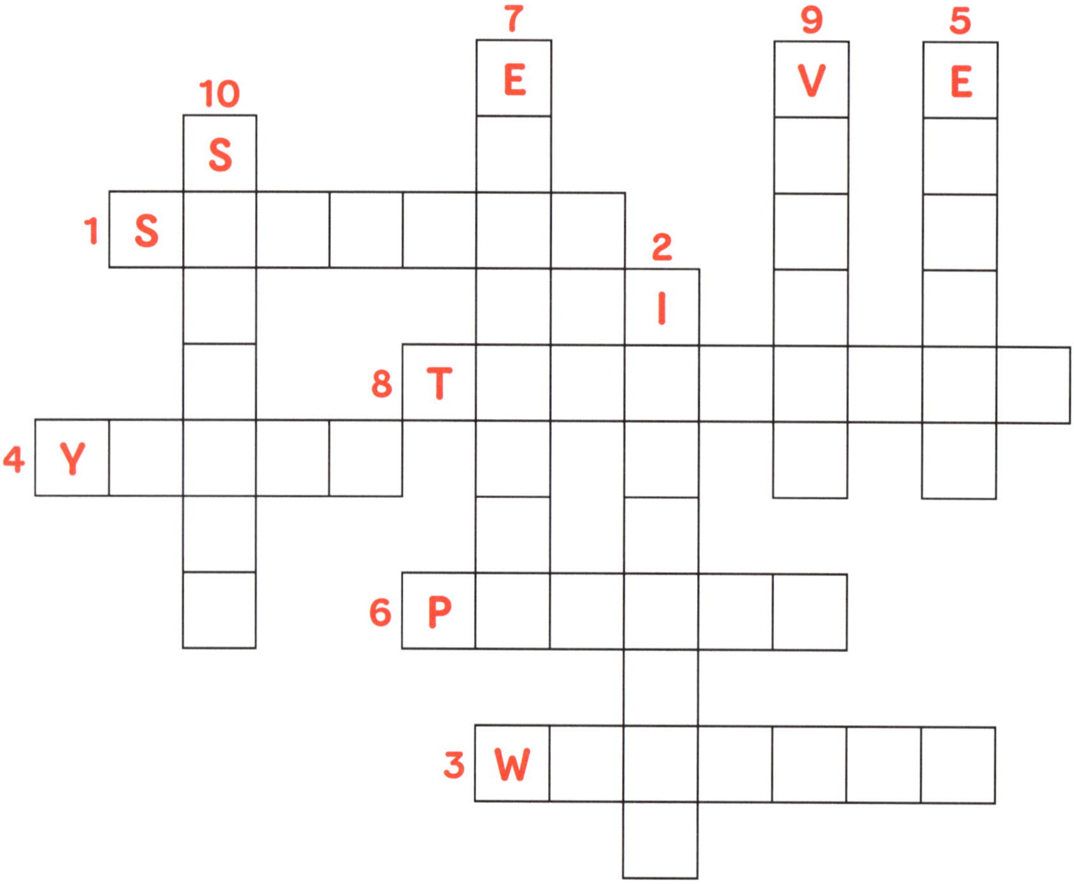

Across	Clue
1	Believe
3	Observe
4	Surrender
6	Opposite of survive
8	Change

Down	Clue
2	To start
5	Tolerate
7	Surround
9	Confirm
10	Halt

Answers: Puzzle Time 10

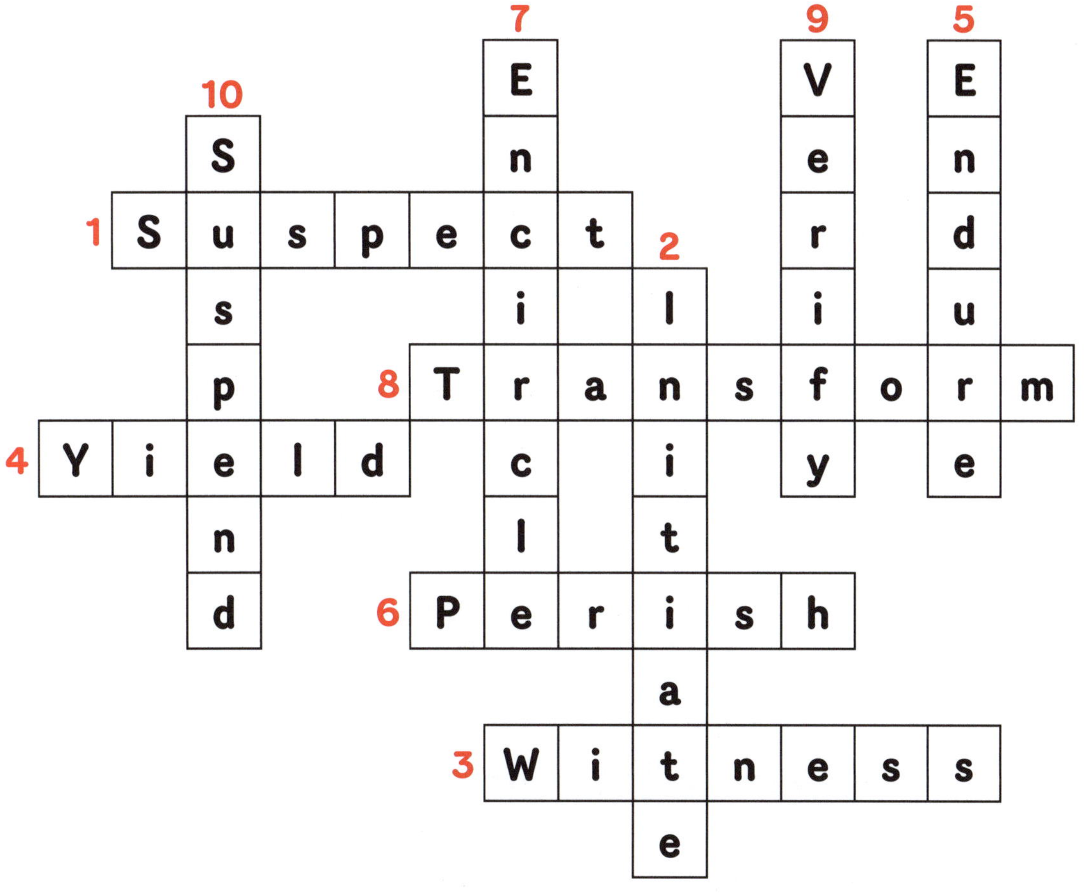

These little marks are tiny yet mighty.

They give sentences their meaning.

Even that little dot –

Don't take it lightly!

Without these little marks,

our sentences have little meaning.

So use our tiny friends

to keep the big thoughts you're gleaning!

CHAPTER 11 Feelings... Whoa, Feelings!

Key Concepts – F. I.L.M.B.E.R.T.

You can make your story more interesting by talking about the characters' thoughts, feelings and actions. Let's look at some of these aspects:

Flow – Control the speed of your narrative to build excitement, tension and intrigue.

Immersion – Pull the reader deeper into the story, making them feel like they're in the story.

Life – Bring the characters to life.

Motivation – What motivates the character? Make the characters' decisions and actions more believable.

Build tension – Make stories more interesting and relatable by describing internal conflict or uncertainties.

Emotional Depth – Add layers of emotion and complexity to experiences.

Relatability – Allow your readers to relate to the characters more personally.

Themes – Highlight underlying themes and messages.

Let's look at some examples for each of these concepts.

Key Concept	Without Description	With Description
Flow	The fight was over.	Amy collapsed to the ground completely exhausted, bleeding from her forehead. She could hear the thunderous cheer of the spectators over the sound of blood pounding in her ears. She could barely see straight, but she didn't mind. She had won and the fight was finally over.
Immersion	Penny was nervous.	Penny could feel her heart beating in her throat. Exhilaration filled the air as the spectators cheered at the sight of their favourite fighters. Penny said a prayer silently and with all her breath and strength, cheered Amy on from the ringside.
Life	Amy was anxious.	Amy's hands trembled, her heart racing as she stepped into the ring. Though the crowd was deafening, she could hear only her heartbeat.
Motivation	Amy wanted to win.	The desire to win a gold medal for the Ultimate Boxing Championship drove Amy to train 12 hours a day for six months. It was her father's dream to become a boxing champion, and it was up to her to fulfil his lost dream.
Build tension	She was afraid.	Amy could feel the knot in her stomach twist tighter. Her opponent was twice her size, and Amy was still recovering from her knee injury. How was she going to beat her?
Emotional Depth	She had a stoic and hard expression.	As Amy looked at her opponent, every cell in her body charged with adrenaline. Yet, she had to keep her gaze still and calm. She could not show her opponent any sign of weakness beneath her stoic exterior.
Relatability	She is a girl who had faced challenges.	Though she lived a comfortable life, Amy always struggled within herself over whether she should box professionally or complete her undergraduate studies. Her parents wanted her to complete her studies and secure her future, but her heart was in boxing and her mind would not let her focus on anything else.
Themes/ Messages	Penny was determined to prove everyone wrong.	All her life, she was told that she did not have a future in contact sports, but Penny knew that even though she could no longer fight, she was a good coach. And through Amy's victory, she would prove that she could indeed have a future in boxing.

Activities

1. Rewriting Thoughts, Feelings and Actions

Using the concepts we explored earlier, rewrite each of the phrases on the left to describe the thought, action or feeling in much more detail. You can decide what the story should be.

Phrase	Story
Don did not want to lose the race.	
Alice was worried.	
Poppins tried to be brave.	
Don walked into the deserted house.	
Poppins was determined.	

2. Bring out the Poet in You!

Select one of the emotions depicted in the four images below and write a poem about it.

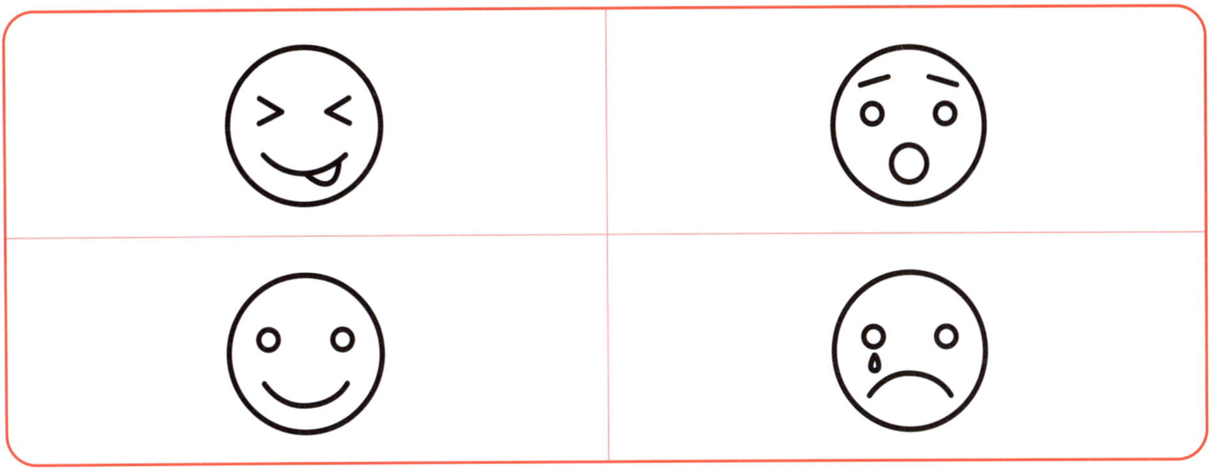

3. Rewrite the Scene

Using the scene prompts below, create your own scenario and make it engaging!

Scene prompt	Your Story Scene
Don is about to direct a movie scene, but feels unprepared.	
Alice walked into the room filled with unfamiliar students.	
Poppins marched out onto the sports track.	
Don went to his favourite restaurant, but they did not have his favourite dish.	
Alice ran towards the Departure Gate to meet her best friend whom she had not seen in three years.	

4. Fill in the Gaps

Write a short paragraph of your own using the dialogue below as a guide. Describe how each character might be feeling, the thoughts they have, and even their actions that follow.

Don: I wish you hadn't said that.

Alice: Why not?

Don: You made her feel lousy.

Alice: You know I did not mean to. I was just telling the truth, and I want her to be prepared.

Don: Yes, but sometimes the truth hurts and it was not the time. She was just getting ready for the race.

Poppins: I'm fine. I don't even care.

Alice: Oh, Poppins! You know I think you're an amazing athlete! I just happened to see Carla training and she was so fast! I have never seen someone that fast.

Don: Alice! That's enough!

Poppins: Just forget it! Both of you, stop it! You're making me more anxious than I was before!

Puzzle Time 11

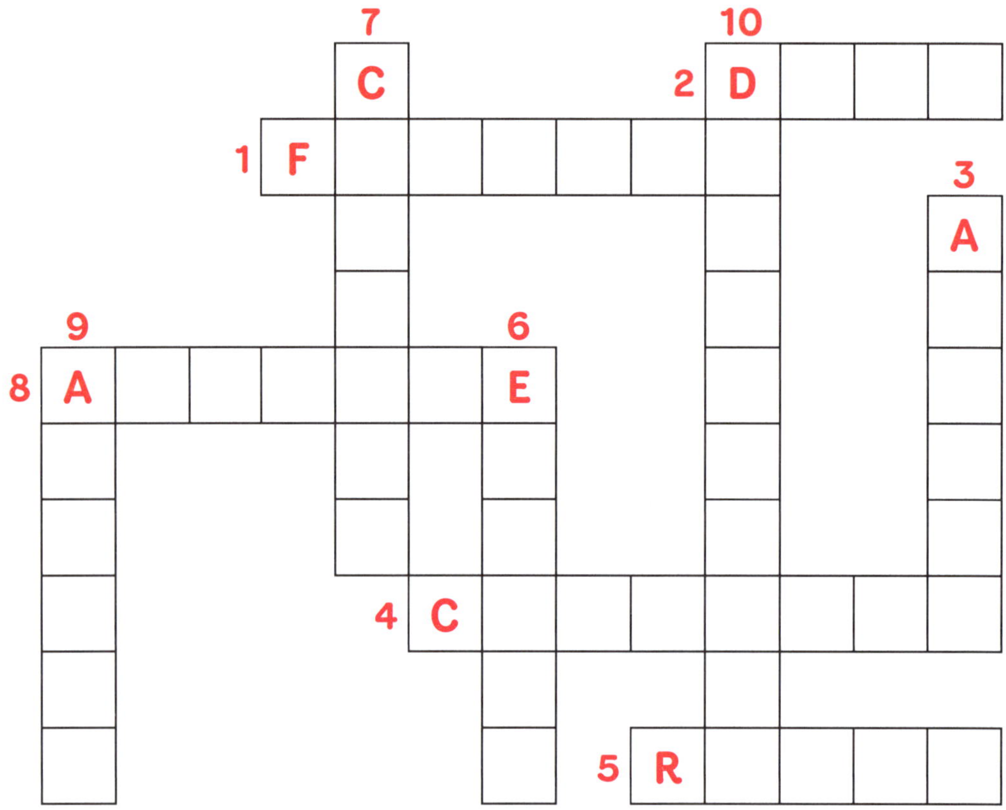

Across	Clue
1	Abandon
2	Opposite of confess
4	Fall
5	Opposite of attract
8	Opposite of fail

Down	Clue
3	Opposite of despise
6	Accompany
7	Praise
9	Adapt
10	To slow down

Answers: Puzzle Time 11

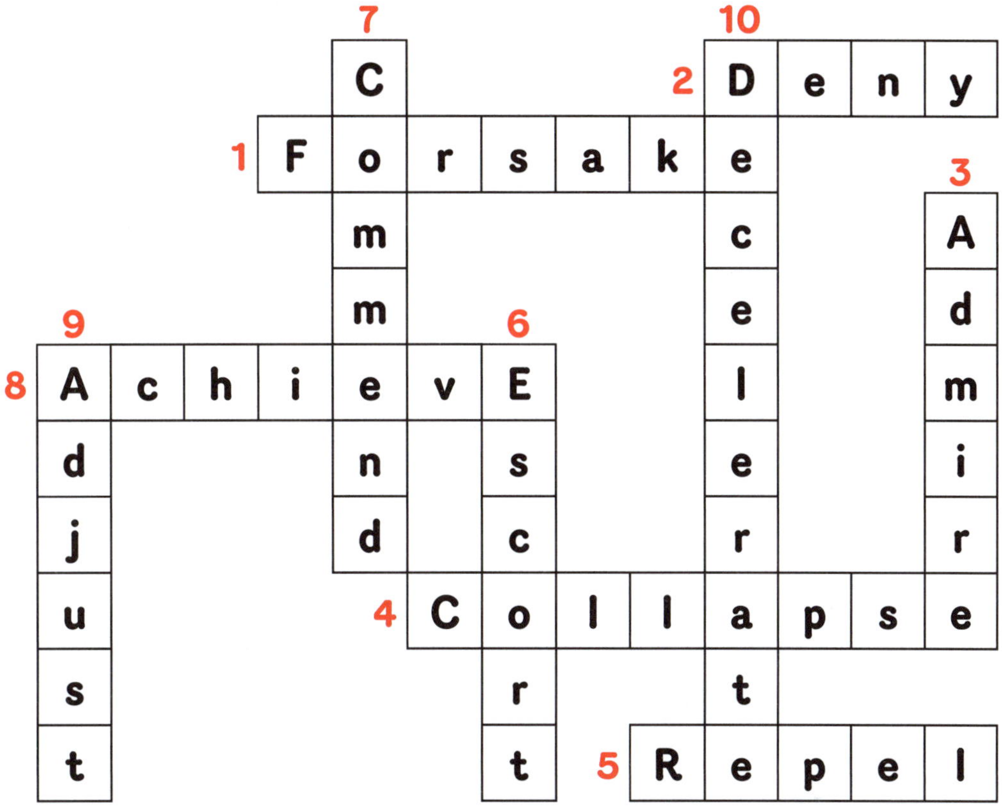

Is your story happy or sad?
Is the character angry or quietly glad?

Are they grateful or excited?
Is their expression gloomy or delighted?

Contented, confused, hopeful or scared?
Oh! Thoughts and feelings,
such treasures to declare!

CHAPTER 12

All's Well That Ends Well

Exactly! A great conclusion can open the door for interpretation. A cliffhanger can keep the reader thinking and imagining about the story!
Whether we choose to end with a cliffhanger or not, we should make sure that the story makes sense and relates back to the important themes. The reader should feel like the journey was worthwhile.
That's true! In art, the negative space (the places left unpainted) can be just as important as the subject itself. Similarly, in writing, what's left unsaid can be powerful.
That's certainly true. However, this is a very difficult skill. There is a difference between your readers feeling a sense of wonder and being confused.
There are some movies where the ending involves a cliffhanger. You know that's when there will probably be a sequel. However, there are some cliffhangers which leave the viewers confused. This is not what we want!
? ? ?
Excellent insights! To create a great conclusion, think about the journey your characters have taken and how they've changed. A good ending should reflect that growth and remind readers of the lessons learned along the way.
We can also use dialogue or internal monologue to express these thoughts in a meaningful way.
Yes! Think about how you want your readers to feel at the end of your story, and use descriptive language to express what they experience, feel or see to create that emotional atmosphere.
Yes! In poetry, imagery can create a sense of completion and fullness that readers will remember long after they finish the story.
So, as you approach your story's conclusion, keep these elements in mind. Reflect on your characters' journeys, reinforce the themes and bring out emotions that resonate with your readers. Your conclusion is the final note in your story's symphony — make it meaningful!
In any wonderful symphony, the key lies in its harmony. After they've journeyed for miles, let it all end with joyous smiles!

Key Concepts

When writing a story, we have learned that there are different parts to consider. Previously, we learned about characters, settings, problems and solutions. Those parts are important to a story. However, it is also important to remember that a meaningful conclusion is a crucial part of the story! It would be a waste to create intriguing characters, wonderful settings, a thoughtful problem and then end with a weak conclusion. A meaningful conclusion is vital to any story, as it leaves the reader with a lasting impression and ties up loose ends.

In addition to wrapping everything up, a well-crafted conclusion may also reinforce the themes, reflect the growth of the characters and give the reader a sense of closure. By providing emotional and narrative satisfaction, a meaningful conclusion helps the story to resonate with readers, leaving them thinking about what they have experienced.

A strong conclusion should resolve the main plot points while showing how the characters have changed. This final part of the story is where everything is connected, revealing what has been learned, achieved or overcome. Whether the ending is happy, sad or bittersweet, it should leave the reader with a sense of completion.

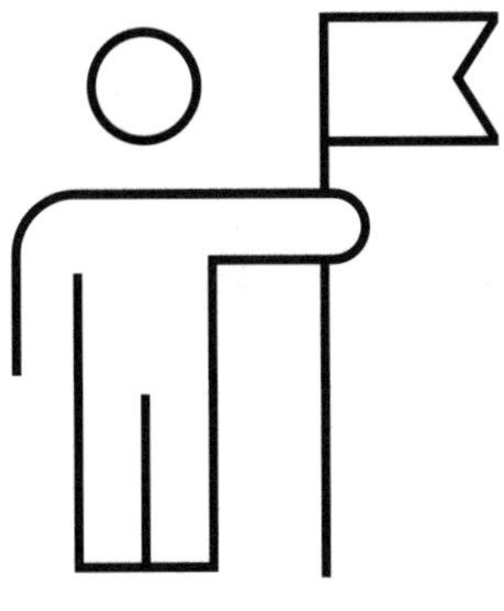

Remember T.I.E.R. to help you craft a meaningful conclusion!

T.I.E.R.

Tie up	In a conclusion, it is vital that you tie up the story by answering the important questions that need to be answered. This gives emotional and narrative closure for the reader. It makes it satisfying for readers to learn how the story concludes meaningfully without any major holes in the plot. **Key questions:** Are the key problems in the story resolved? Are there any unanswered questions at the end of the story? If there isn't a sequel, is there a sense of closure at the end of the story?
Impact	By the end of the story, the characters' actions in overcoming the problem may have had an impact on the larger world beyond themselves. **Key questions:** What lasting impact does the main event of the story leave? Has anything been changed? What is it? How will the characters' lives be different?
Evolution	A character will change through the course of the story and the events that happen. It is important to show and acknowledge this in a conclusion. **Key questions:** How has the character changed from the start to end of the story? What important lesson did the characters learn? How will they apply it?
Reflection	In a conclusion, it is important to go back and reflect on the key themes/values/ideas that were highlighted in the story. These themes or ideas form the key message the writer wants the readers to take with them after they finish reading the story. **Key questions:** What message do I want the reader to think about after the story ends? How does my conclusion highlight this key message? How do the characters reflect on their growth and journey? What does the character's growth mean for their future?

T.I.E.R. in Action!

Example story:

In a mystical forest, a young boy named Liam goes on a journey to find a hidden cure for a mysterious illness that is spreading through his village. Along the way, he encounters magical creatures, overcomes dangerous obstacles and faces his own fears. In the end, Liam discovers that the cure he seeks is not a potion, herb or spell, but the power of hope and belief in the villagers themselves.

See the table below as an example of how you can apply **T.I.E.R.** to create a meaningful conclusion.

Follow Alice as she crafts a meaningful conclusion!

Tie up	**Key question:** How is the main problem in the story resolved? **Possible answer:** The main problem of finding a cure for the village's illness is resolved when Liam realises that the cure was giving his fellow villagers hope and belief in themselves. **Key question:** Are there any character arcs that need to be tied up? **Possible answer:** No. Liam's character arc is fully completed as he has overcome his fear and self-doubt, gaining the courage to inspire others. **Key question:** Have the different story ideas been tied up in a satisfying way that feels complete? **Possible answer:** Yes. The mysterious illness is cured, and Liam returns to his village as a brave hero. Apart from healing the people, he has brought a new sense of unity and strength to the entire village.
Impact	**Key question:** What lasting impact does the main event in the story have on the main characters and their world? **Possible answer:** The villagers are now stronger as a community because they have learned to believe in their own resilience rather than relying on mystical magic. **Key question:** How will the main characters' lives be different after the story ends? **Possible answer:** Liam was once a quiet boy who was unsure of himself. At the end of the story, he becomes a respected leader in the village and a symbol of hope and bravery.

Evolution	**Key question:** How has the main character changed from the beginning to the end of the story? **Possible answer:** Liam has grown from a fearful, uncertain boy in the beginning into a confident and brave leader, who now understands that true power comes from within. **Key question:** What important lesson did the character learn, and how will he/she apply it in the future? **Possible answer:** Liam learns that hope and belief are the key values to have. In the future, he will continue to inspire others by spreading this message. **Key question:** Does my conclusion show the growth of the characters in a meaningful way? **Possible answer:** Yes. The conclusion highlights Liam's evolution, showing how his internal growth led to external change in the village.
Reflection	**Key question:** What key message or idea do I want my readers to think about after the story ends? **Possible answer:** The key message of the story is that true strength and healing come from within, and that belief in oneself and in others can overcome even the most difficult obstacles. **Key question:** How does my conclusion reinforce the key message of my story? **Possible answer:** The conclusion reinforces the key message by showing how the mysterious illness was not cured by magic, potions or herbs. It was cured by the power of hope, something that everyone in the village can tap into.

Alice's conclusion:

Liam's journey taught him that magic, potions or herbs are not the answer to everything, as the cure to the mysterious illness in his village was to give his fellow villagers the power of hope. Through his struggles with magical creatures, difficult obstacles and his own fear and doubt, the villagers saw Liam's hopefulness and resilience. They took inspiration from him, and immediately started feeling better. As the mysterious illness spread through his village, Liam's curiosity and quick thinking helped him find a cure just in time. Though he doubted himself at first, his courage grew as he solved each puzzle. By the end, Liam was no longer the uncertain boy he once was — he had become the village's quiet hero. The experience gave him the strength to trust in his instincts, knowing that even the smallest of steps can make a huge difference.

T.I.E.R. in Action!

Example story:
In a magical kingdom, a young girl named Aria needs to save her village from a terrible drought. She goes on a journey. Along the way, she meets an enchanted river spirit who offers her three riddles to solve. If she answers them correctly, the spirit will guide her to a hidden spring deep within the mountains that can restore water to her land. Throughout her journey, Aria learns the value of patience, wisdom, and the strength of community.

Poppins needs some help! Use **T.I.E.R.** to help her in crafting a meaningful conclusion!

Tie up	**Key question:** How is the main problem in the story resolved? The main problem is resolved when ____________________ ____________________ **Key question:** Are there any character arcs that need to be tied up? Through Aria's personal journey of overcoming her challenge, she ____________________ ____________________.
Impact	**Key question:** What lasting impact does the main event in the story have on the main characters and their world? The villagers now ____________________ ____________________ ____________________ **Key question:** How will the main characters' lives be different after the story ends? The main characters' lives are different because ____________________ ____________________ ____________________.

Evolution	**Key question:** How has the main character changed from the beginning to the end of the story? Aria begins the story as ______________________ ______________________ In the end, Aria ______________________ ______________________ **Key question:** What important lesson did the character learn, and how will he/she apply it in the future? Aria learns the importance of ______________________ ______________________.
Reflection	**Key question:** What key message or idea do I want my readers to think about after the story ends? The key message of the story is that ______________________ ______________________. **Key question:** How does my conclusion reinforce the key message of my story? The conclusion reinforces the key message by ______________________ ______________________.

Poppins' conclusion

As Aria stood before the villagers, holding a jar of clear water from the hidden spring, she felt a wave of relief wash over her. It had been a long and difficult journey, but she had done it. The drought was over. Her village would once again thrive. However, it was more than just restoring life to her village. Aria knew she had changed from within. Solving the river spirit's riddles had taught her the value of patience and the power of a calm, thoughtful mind. No longer the impulsive girl who rushed into things, Aria had become a wise leader. She had become someone the villagers could rely on. She looked out at the smiling faces of her people, knowing that this wasn't just about finding water. It was about finding strength in herself and in her community. From that day forward, they would all work together, not just for the next rainy season, but for a future filled with hope and resilience.

Possible answers

Tie up	**Key question:** How is the main problem in the story resolved? **Possible answer:** The main problem is resolved when Aria is able to figure out the answers to the riddles, allowing her to eventually restore water to her land. **Key question:** Are there any character arcs that need to be tied up? **Possible answer:** Through Aria's personal journey of overcoming her challenge, she learns the value of patience and to think things through calmly.
Impact	**Key question:** What lasting impact does the main event in the story have on the main characters and their world? **Possible answer:** The villagers now have access to water again, which means they will be able to survive and thrive. **Key question:** How will the main characters' lives be different after the story ends? **Possible answer:** The main characters' lives are different because they now look forward to the future with hope and resilience, no matter what difficulties may arise.
Evolution	**Key question:** How has the main character changed from the beginning to the end of the story? **Possible answer:** Aria begins the story as an impatient and impulsive girl. In the end, Aria becomes a more patient and thoughtful person. **Key question:** What important lesson did the character learn, and how will he/she apply it in the future? **Possible answer:** Aria learns the importance of being patient, to think things through carefully before one acts and the importance of serving one's community.
Reflection	**Key question:** What key message or idea do I want my readers to think about after the story ends? **Possible answer:** The key message of the story is that it is important to act for the greater good. **Key question:** How does my conclusion reinforce the key message of my story? **Possible answer:** The conclusion reinforces the key message by emphasising how the community's well-being and sense of unity are crucial.

T.I.E.R. in Action!

Story:

14-year-old Emma had always been passionate about music and dreamt of winning the school talent show. She spent weeks perfecting her song on the piano and felt that anything short of winning the talent show would be failure. The night before the big day, her sheet music was accidentally ruined, leaving her without the notes she had carefully prepared. This made her feel overwhelmed and caused her to doubt her ability to perform the songs she had prepared. Emma was distraught and considered withdrawing. However, her supportive older brother and her music teacher encouraged her. Emma learnt that true talent came from within. She also learnt that the real prize was something within herself, rather than an object given by someone else.

See the table below to practise applying **T.I.E.R.** to create a meaningful conclusion!

Tie up	How is the main problem in the story resolved? __________ __________ __________ Are there any character arcs that need to be tied up? __________ __________ __________
Impact	What is the impact of the events in the story on the main characters and their world? __________ __________ __________ How will the main characters' lives be different after the story ends? __________ __________ __________

Evolution	How has the main character changed from the beginning to the end of the story? __________ __________ __________ What important lesson did the character learn, and how will he/she apply it in the future? __________ __________ __________
Reflection	What key message or idea do I want my readers to think about after the story ends? __________ __________ __________ How does my conclusion reinforce the key message of my story? __________ __________

In the space below, use your responses in the **T.I.E.R.** table above to write your meaningful conclusion!

Puzzle Time 12

Across	Clue
1	Explain
3	Complain
5	Opposite of gather
6	Opposite of compete
9	Evaluate

Down	Clue
2	Opposite of descend
4	Assess
7	Combine
8	Boast
10	Focus

Answers: Puzzle Time 12

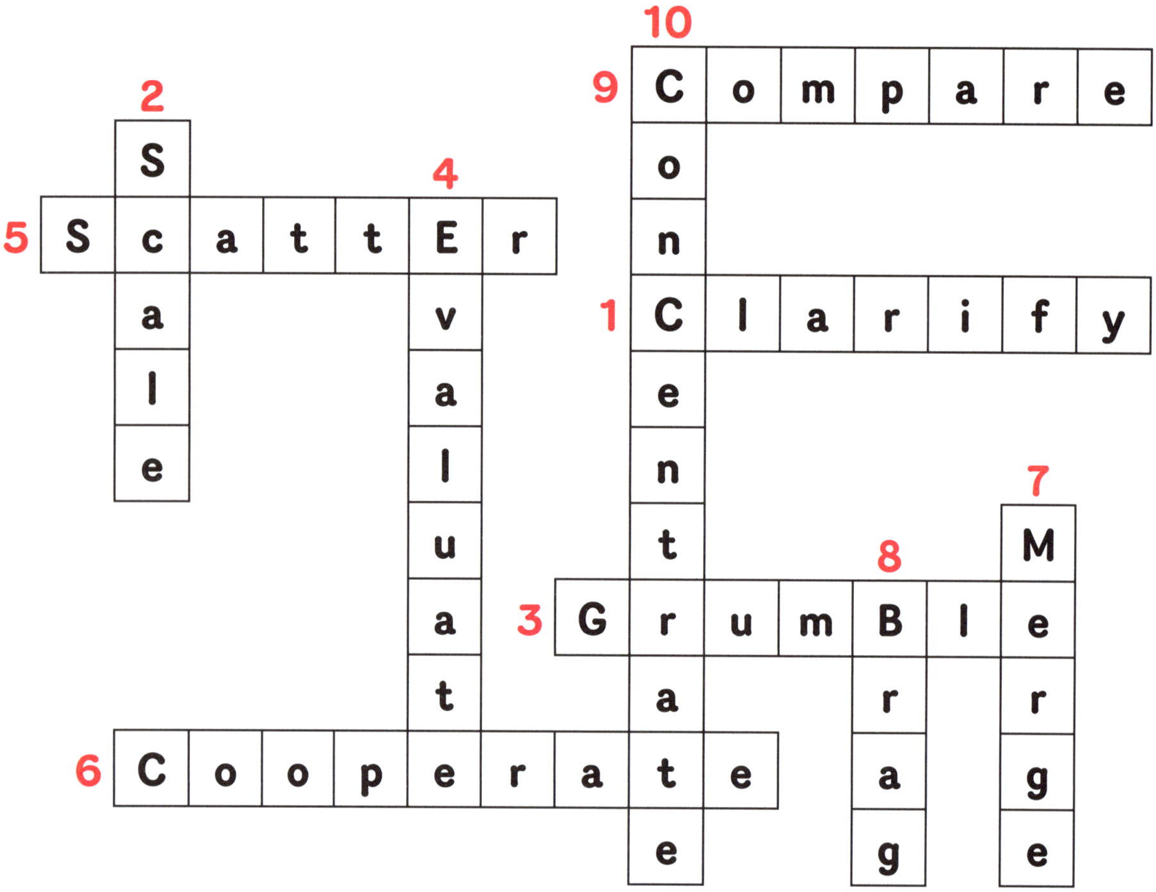

A story's end, a final bow,
it wraps up all we've learned till now.
With threads tied tight, and lessons clear,
a meaningful close draws us near.

The hero's growth, the battles won,
reflections cast when all is done.
Their journey lingers in our mind,
a lasting truth for us to find.

So, write an end both strong and true,
that echoes long past what we knew.
A thoughtful end will always stay,
in hearts and minds, well on its way.

Read the rest of the series!

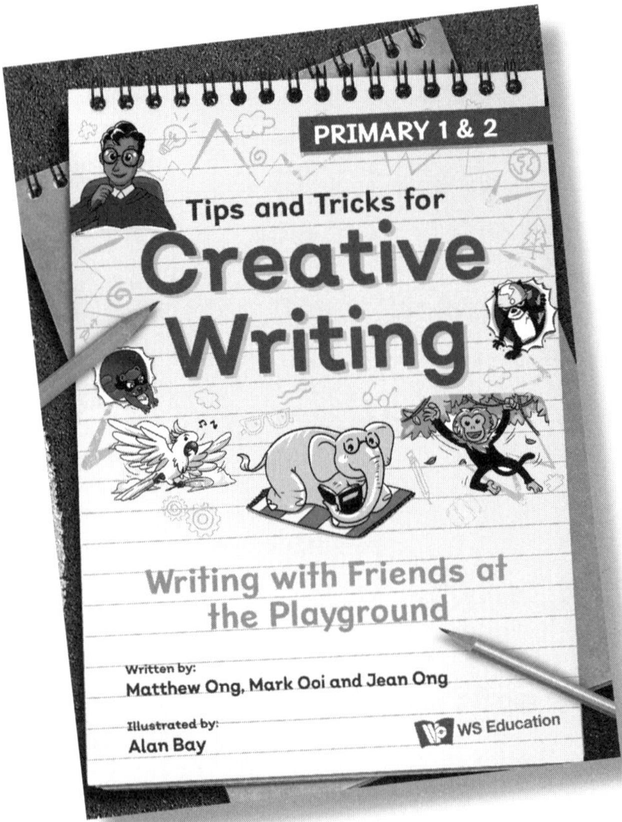

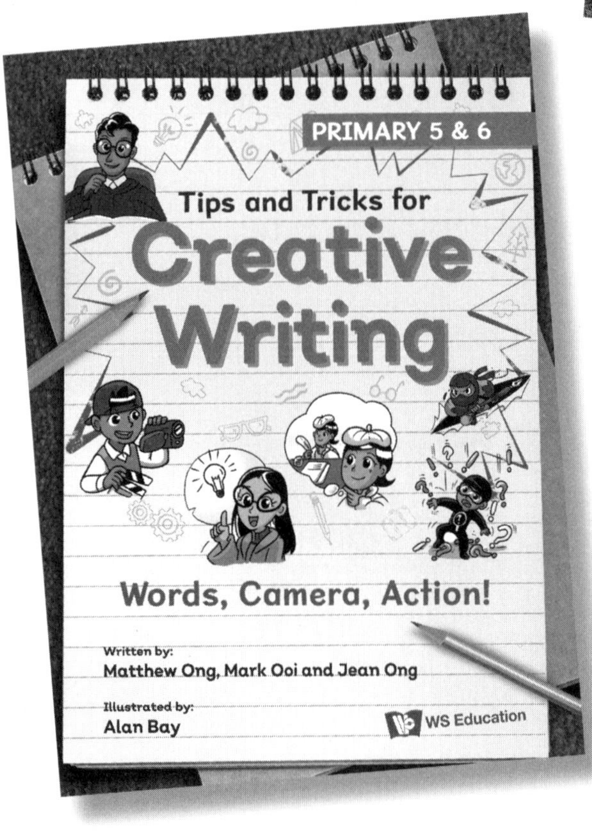

To receive updates about children's titles from WS Education, go to **https://www.worldscientific.com/page/newsletter/subscribe**, choose "Education", click on "Children's Books" and key in your email address.

WS Education